Hattie's Book

A Woman's Life in a City's History

By

Beverly Jane Phillips

Chicago: Paul Bechtold Library Publications
Catholic Theological Union
2019

Copyright © Beverly Jane Phillips. 2019.

This work is licensed under a Creative Commons Attribution-NonCommercial-No-Derivatives 3.0 License. Please contact **pblpubs@ctu.edu** to use this work in a way not covered by the license. The print version of this book is available for sale from Amazon/CreateSpace.

Published 2019 by

Paul Bechtold Library Publications
Catholic Theological Union
5401 S. Cornell Ave.
Chicago, IL 60615

pblpubs@ctu.edu

Focus and Scope: Paul Bechtold Library Publications is a Catholic online, open-access publisher of theology and pastoral ministry monographs at the Catholic Theological Union through the Paul Bechtold Library. Its mission is to serve the Church by providing a forum for theologians and pastoral ministers to engage the Catholic tradition in respectful, constructive, and critical dialogue. Its primary intent and direction is to promote a deeper understanding of the Christian faith and the mission of the Church.

The mission of Catholic Theological Union is to prepare effective leaders for the Church, ready to witness to Christ's good news of justice, love, and peace.

Cover designed by Holly Silcox
Cover Photo of Hattie Williams used by permission: Chicago History Museum.

Library of Congress Cataloging-in-Publication Data

Names: Phillips, Beverly Jane, author.

Title: Hattie's book : a woman's life in a city's history / by Beverly Jane Phillips.

Description: Chicago, IL : Paul Bechtold Library Publications, Catholic Theological Union, 2019. | Includes bibliographical references.

Identifiers: ISBN 9780963665973 (print) | ISBN 9780963665980 (ebook)

Subjects: Williams, Hattie Kay, 1922-1990. | Women, Black—Biography. | Catholic women—Biography. | African American social workers—Illinois—Chicago—Biography. | Community activists—Illinois—Chicago—Biography. | African American political activists—Illinois—Chicago—Biography. | Educational equalization—Illinois—Chicago.

Classification: LCC BX4705.W55 P45 2019

I have learned that people are people and that compassion is in the heart of every human being if you learn to communicate with them. I have learned to have faith in God and I have learned that God can open doors that we are unable to see.

Hattie Kay Williams

Table of Contents

Preface/Introduction   i-iv

1 Meeting Hattie   1

2 Hattie's Life   9

3 Race Riot   30

4 Bronzeville/Oakland   36

5 Shalom Community   45

6 Public Housing   54

7 Babies Having Babies   70

8 Public Schools   86

9 Politics   121

10 Hattie's Prayers   130

Appendices   139

Acknowledgements   152

Bibliography   154

PREFACE

There are rare times when you meet someone whom you recognize immediately as an especially unique person. Such was my experience the first time I met Hattie Williams. It was in her home in the ghetto, called Bronzeville on the South Side of Chicago. In 1988 Hattie asked me to write a book about her life and work in the ghetto. I promised her I would. She died in 1990. All we had done towards her book was two conversations which centered on what she wanted to say in her book. To supplement those conversations she gave me 38 typed, double-spaced pages that were transcripts of tapes recorded by Betsy Edwards, another friend of Hattie. The conversations were unfinished. She also gave me the transcript of another interview which was conducted many years before by a friend who was a priest. This transcript is much briefer and is also incomplete.

To my knowledge there has been no book has been written about Hattie but there needs to be. She was a remarkable woman in her faith and in her actions. History is peopled by black women like Hattie who are remarkable in strength and determination, in their faith, in their works, and in their service to people around them. This book is my attempt to keep my promise to Hattie and to honor her memory; to tell the story of her life and also the story of the institutional racism that she faced as she worked to make life better for her neighbors in the ghetto.

INTRODUCTION

Stories about Hattie's good works and her answered prayers abound. When I began writing this book to keep my promise to Hattie I imagined that it would be a book of those anecdotes. Very soon I realized that in order to honor Hattie, to do justice to who she was, I needed to know more about her neighborhood in Chicago. Her immediate neighborhood was Oakland, but the whole area has various names: Bronzeville, the Black Belt, the Black Metropolis.

She could be described simply as a church lady in the best sense of that label. Hattie believed strongly that God was active in her life and in the world. Her faith led her to make lasting relationships with individuals, Christian churches, colleges and seminaries. Having been brought up in a devout Pentecostal family she was also enriched by being active in a Baptist church and then in the Roman Catholic Church. As she went about doing good in her poverty-stricken neighborhood she often said, "God opens doors where there are no doors. He makes a way where there is no way."

Gathering stories about her involvement in her neighborhood I soon discovered that in addition to doing good as a "church lady" she was a strong and determined activist in the efforts to achieve equality for black people. It became patently obvious that telling Hattie's story meant delving into the actions of the powers and principalities of her time, the politics of local, state, and federal governments. The policies of these governments and the people who had the power in them purposefully resulted in laws and practices which contributed to the oppression and poverty not only of blacks but all people of color.

Thus began almost a decade of reading and studying about the oppression of black Chicagoans in housing, in education, and in employment. I can't claim academic degrees in the history, the politics, or the sociology of race relations in Chicago but in these years of writing *Hattie's Book* I have read a long and extensive list of books and articles on the subject of the treatment of black people in Chicago. My research has consisted of finding at least two sources that verify what I have written. As with any topic the opinions of observers are not unanimous. I have tried to express the viewpoint of events that Hattie held. My research continued even as the last draft of the book was in its final stages. The bibliography contains the names of the books and articles that were most helpful to me and to which I referred over and over again.

One of the many things I discovered during my research was that many strong women, both black and white, fought the fight in which Hattie was engaged. My hope is that Hattie will be honored not only by what she did but also by being shown to be at home on any list of powerful, dedicated, and determined women.

Two things need some explanation. One is the names of the area and the other is the use of the word "black."

Because they are used interchangeably it is necessary to explain the various names given to the South Side black ghetto of Chicago where Hattie lived and served her whole life. The "Black Belt" is the most prominent name given to the area of Chicago on the South Side. It was sometimes called the "Black Metropolis." There are smaller enclaves of black people in other areas, mostly on the West Side of the city. However, by the middle of the twentieth century three quarters of the black population of Chicago lived in the Black Belt which stretched for thirty blocks along State Street south from 39th Street to 95th Street between the Dan Ryan Expressway and Lake Michigan.

Another name, commonly used today, for the area was Bronzeville. This name was suggested by the owner of the black newspaper, *The Chicago Defender*, and was readily accepted by the people living there. In fact the people came to celebrate that name with a yearly election of a "mayor" and a parade. Within the Black Belt are several neighborhoods. The northern most was Oakland which was where Hattie's home was. Side by side with Oakland the communities of North Kenwood and Kenwood extended to south to the borders of Hyde Park.

I have consistently referred to the people about whom I am writing as "blacks" or "black people." Most of my sources use that term although some use "Negro" and some use "African-American." The changing of names can be a source of confusion not only for people who are white but also for people who are black. One of Hattie's elderly neighbor women was showing me her narrow back-yard garden one day. It was lush with collard greens and mustard greens with not a weed to be found. She explained that black people like to eat greens. "We have been called Negro, black, African-American. I don't know what they call us now, but whatever it is we do like these greens."

More and more as I have worked on *Hattie's Book* I have become aware that as a white woman I am treading on thin ice. The possibility of insulting good people, the danger of conveying racist ideas, looms large. When I was a child and ever since, I have been open and accepting of any people of any color. Having said that I acknowledge that the racism that pollutes the very air we breathe in the United States has no doubt found a lodging place in my heart and mind. Hopefully it is a very small place and someday it and all racism will be erased.

Chapter 1
MEETING HATTIE

We drove up in two cars and parked on the street in front of a three-story Victorian-style house in a row of Victorian houses built in the 1880s. The neighborhood was called by various names: Kenwood/Oakland, the Black Belt, the Black Metropolis, and Bronzeville. We arrived there by driving south on Lake Shore Drive, exiting at 35th Street and turning south on South Lake Park Avenue. It was a route that gave us only a glimpse of the poverty and devastation we were about to enter.

The "we" who arrived in front of Hattie's house were the Hunger Committee of the Presbytery of Chicago. The year was 1981. The work of our committee was to educate the members of 138 Presbyterian churches in the Chicago area about hunger and poverty. Our goal was not just to talk about these issues, but also to do something to alleviate them. All of us were privileged, not necessarily affluent, but privileged white women.

Rather than just talk about conditions of poverty in Chicago, we decided we needed to see it firsthand. The dedicated, intense moderator of the committee, Gladys Leininger, had met Hattie Kay Williams at a meeting and learned about the work she was doing in the ghetto, which had been her home since her birth there in 1922 until she died in 1990.

Part of Hattie's mission in life was to invite people from the "outside" not only to witness the poverty of her people but also to do something about it. It was a perfect setup for us to visit in order to give substance and meaning to our work as a committee dedicated to alleviating hunger and poverty. Hattie's plan included taking people like us on walking tours of the area.

When we knocked on her door, Hattie greeted us and led us into her living room. At the risk of offending anyone who knew her and her home, I will say that her house was rundown. It was not ramshackle, but it had been and was being well used. Hattie raised six children in this three-thousand-square-foot, fifteen-room, home that she owned. Housing that many children would be enough to wear down any house, let alone one that was approaching its one-hundredth birthday, having been built in 1888. Added to very normal wear and tear was the steady traffic of all the people who entered there for the myriad of activities hosted by Hattie.

One example of hard use was the time an Illinois farmer offered her one hundred chickens to distribute to her hungry neighbors. She gladly accepted the offer not knowing until they arrived that these would be one hundred *live* chickens! The chickens spent the night in her dining room! Hattie, being a city woman, had no idea how awful a room full of chickens could be. When morning came, friends and neighbors flooded in to claim the chickens, each family being left to their own devices as to how to deal with a live chicken they looked forward to eating. That experience caused her to declare that she would never do that again even though it provided much-needed food for hungry people.

It was a given that when you went to Hattie's you would be involved in prayer at least once during your visit. To an interior designer, her small living room would have had too many chairs. Hattie arranged it that way on purpose. In that room, it was possible for a group of people to hold hands in a circle of prayer without reaching or straining. The very minute she started praying, something like an electric current flowed through the circle. The Holy Spirit flowed from person to person around the circle, uniting us with God and with Hattie in the search for justice for all people in the ghetto and in the white communities that impacted the ghetto.

As Hattie prayed with the six of us from the Hunger Committee, we all knew immediately that we were in the presence of a holy person. She had become a Roman Catholic, but she prayed with all the fervor of a Pentecostal, which was the faith in which she had been raised. Her prayers even reached into the environment around her. Once when she and I were praying alone together, her baby canary began to sing. She stopped praying and we just listened to the sparkling cascades of notes. Then she said, "He is too young to sing." Hattie's prayers brought out the music of the Holy Spirit wherever and whenever she uttered them.

After she spoke to us for a while about the problems of people in the ghetto, we set out on a walking tour of the area, our destination being

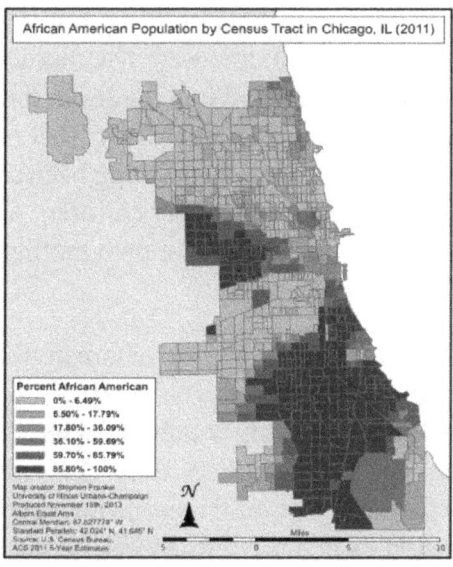

African American Population by Census Tract in Chicago (2011), 2013. Map credit: Stephen Frankel.

the home of a single mother and her six children. As we walked, we found ourselves in the reality of poverty that we had only heard about. Lake Shore Drive, a beautiful urban parkway that extends from north to south along the shore of Lake Michigan, gave no hint of the devastation and poverty that lay just west of it. The area looked like a bombed European city during World War II. We saw empty lots filled with trash and debris of all kinds, remains of burned-out buildings, and dilapidated houses in which people still lived at the risk of their health and even their lives.

We walked several blocks and arrived at a three-story brick tenement that stood alone in a field of vacant lots, crumbled sidewalks, and decaying streets. The building had six apartments. The day we visited there were two families living in two of the apartments, while the others were vacant. The gas to the building had been cut off and the elevator no longer worked. The mother of the woman we were visiting had died in her daughter's third-floor apartment. She was a large woman, which made it impossible for the firefighters who came for her body to get it down the steep, narrow steps. So they moved a ladder truck with a basket to the side of the building and brought her body down in the basket.

After climbing the dirty, broken, and chipped marble steps to the third floor we entered a small apartment that was immaculately clean. A woman who looked older than her age and her six carefully groomed children between the ages of two and fourteen greeted us. After Hattie made introductions we took seats in the living room while the children scattered themselves among us. At Hattie's prompting, this single mother began to tell us her story.

There were four men involved in the births of these children but not one of them was currently on the scene to help in any way. The mother explained that each time she met a man who flattered her, made her feel loved, and professed to love her children, she had another baby. That or something else caused the men to move on. She regretted having been so naïve, but at the same time, she dearly loved each one of her children. As a result, she was a single mother who, since the death of her own mother, had no one to help her take care of the children.

Then as now, people in power and people in general blame welfare mothers for laziness and ignorance as causes of their poverty. After all, the reasoning goes, they should get a job and support themselves instead of relying on taxpayers to support them and their children. It never seems to occur to the people in power that there may be valid reasons for a person not to work. This single mother told us that she didn't work because if she worked her children would not go to school. Then they would end up just like her. If she had a job, she would have to leave before they did in the morning. Because of a lack of jobs in the nearby area, she would have to take public transportation to and from a job, which would most likely be in the suburbs. The children would be left to get themselves ready for school and out the door to school. Maybe they would go to school and maybe they wouldn't. Besides leaving before they awoke in the mornings, she would get home after they got home from school and they would be without supervision. It is easy to imagine the trouble children could get into in such a situation. Quite often welfare mothers are berated and even prosecuted for leaving children alone, but sometimes they have no alternatives.

As we sat in the family's living room listening to the mother's story, a woman on the committee suddenly gave a squeal and straightened her legs to raise her feet off the floor. She had seen a rat run across the floor in the kitchen. Our host explained that it was routine that rats chewed holes by the kitchen window and came in. She repeatedly stuffed the holes with steel wool, but the rats chewed new holes right beside the old ones and boldly came right in.

At the end of our visit, Hattie gathered us all into a circle of prayer, and we all held hands. Hattie held my right hand and one of the little girls, a beautiful, bright-eyed five-year-old, held my left hand. When Hattie finished praying she very quietly called my attention to the little girl's hand clasped in mine. Her fingers were webbed. Only the very tips of her fingers were visible beyond the webbing. It became clear immediately that with this disability this precious child would not only have difficulties picking up and holding things but also would suffer curious notice from adults and ridicule from children.

When we were back in Hattie's living room, she explained that this mother had very little food to eat during her pregnancy with this child—mostly she drank tea. The mother's malnutrition was the cause of the webbing of her little daughter's hand. Even though she had just met us, Hattie was not shy about asking if there was any way we could provide medical care that might include surgery to remove the webbing. The first thought I had was the Shriners Hospital for Children in Chicago and all the free medical work they do for children. Part of the hospital's mission is to provide the highest quality care to children with special health care needs, among them orthopedic needs. Charges are based on the family's ability to pay. Hattie was excited about this possibility, so she asked if we could inquire about the hospital to helping this little girl by doing corrective surgery on her hand.

By making several phone calls, we were able to get the little girl accepted for an evaluation at the hospital with surgery to follow. The staff assured us they could make her hand be more functional and look better. All the mother had to do was take her to the hospital for evaluation and follow up. When we shared this good news with Hattie, she advised that from then on we should let the mother take the initiative for appointments and follow up. The mother never followed through even though the surgery and treatment were free and her daughter's hand would be repaired. She was afraid for her child and for herself. Hattie explained that the mother was fearful because they would have to ride buses or trains for eight miles through several areas of Chicago to the hospital, which was on the Near North Side. She was afraid because white riders would be riding the trains and buses, and she and her daughter would be passing through white neighborhoods. Maybe more importantly, she was afraid of having white people take care of her daughter. Her fear was based on the dangers white people represented in her own personal experience and in the history of black people in the United States.[1]

---

1 At the time, this seemed to me like cowardice and gross neglect on the mother's part. However, since I have been doing research for this book, I have come to realize that her fears were grounded in the real-life treatment of black people by white people.

The Hunger Committee left this experience more determined than ever to put all its efforts into helping make things better for poor families. We had seen firsthand what we had preached and taught about—that the plight of so many poor people is the fault of a flawed system as much as or more than it is an individual's fault.

From that day in 1980 to Hattie's death in 1990, she and her ministry became a part of the life of my family and of the life of the church of which my husband was the pastor, Christ Presbyterian (USA) Church in Hanover Park, Illinois, a northwest suburb of Chicago. My husband, Norm, and our teenage children, Jim and Nancy, made many trips to Hattie's house in the Oakland/Kenwood neighborhood about thirty miles from our home. Several people from the church made trips there as well, but most of the church people were afraid to go to Hattie's because it was in a gang-ridden, dangerous area. However, even the people who were afraid to make deliveries in person helped by donating money, food, clothing, and furniture.

All of us also engaged in garbage picking. On the day the garbage containers were set out in our white suburbs we would cruise the streets looking for good stuff that Hattie's people could use. She encouraged us to bring everything we found and she would decide what was usable and what was not. The most disgusting things she wanted were mattresses. Most of the ones we found were stained with urine and vomit as well as having the stuffing sticking out from jagged tears. But even those rejects were better than what many people in Hattie's neighborhood had. There were whole families who slept on the floor on piles of their dirty clothes. When washday came the clothes disappeared and the bare floor was where they slept until more dirty clothes accumulated to become their beds.

Sometimes when we took large items to Hattie we called her to tell her what we were bringing and she would have people waiting who needed what we brought. One day we had a particularly disgusting mattress. When we arrived at Hattie's, a woman and her small son were waiting with a grocery cart in the front yard. They loaded the mattress onto the cart and headed down the street with the mom pushing the cart and the little boy keeping it balanced.

Yard and garage sales were rich sources for meeting the needs of poor people in the ghetto. Christ Church people went to these sales at the end of the day and told them what they wanted and who it was for. More times than not, the sellers would bundle up whatever remained and just give it to them. Often what was left over was baby clothes, for which Hattie had great need. She never had enough clothes for the "babies being born to babies," the teenage mothers for whom Hattie had a heart-rending concern.

Our opportunities to go into the homes of the people took two forms. One was when we had furniture to deliver and the other was special donations of food. Once when we had chairs, dressers, and lamps to deliver, Hattie sent us to an apartment on the fifteenth floor of one of the public housing buildings across the street from her home. We loaded the furniture and ourselves into the filthy elevator and looked for the button for the fifteenth floor. That stop was out of order. The elevator stopped at the fourteenth and the sixteenth but not at the fifteenth. Making the decision that it would be easier to carry the stuff up than down, we unloaded on the fourteenth floor and carried the furniture up a narrow flight of smelly, dirty stairs.

As I got to know Hattie and the challenges she and her neighbors faced I found answers to questions that had plagued me throughout my growing-up years. I was born and raised in Hastings, Nebraska, a small town which during World War II became a microcosm of Chicago. When the Department of the Navy built an ammunitions plant in Hastings, the town changed drastically. Before the building of the Navy Ammunition Depot, the population was made up of white people of European descent with just a sprinkling of people of color. When construction of the Depot began in 1942, hundreds and hundreds of nonwhite people moved or were moved to town, causing a serious housing problem. Some Sioux Indians came to work there and lived in tents right on Depot land, but so many blacks came that the city designated special places for them to live. Hundreds of them lived in a development of motel-type structures built especially for them and in several trailer parks and campgrounds.

The questions, actually judgments, asked even after the Navy Depot closed in 1949 were these: Why don't black people take care of the places where they live? Why do they cluster together in small areas? Why do they have so many children? Why don't they take advantage of opportunities that come along? Why are they afraid of white people? These judgments are still made by white Americans today.

My experiences with Hattie and my research for this book have answered some of those questions and have shown them to be not just innocent questions but harsh, uninformed judgments. Hattie knew the answers to these questions because she lived them and faced them every day of her life. Her response was to help people live as well as they could in spite of the constraints put on them from many sources.

Hattie knew the answers.

Chapter 2
HATTIE'S LIFE

Hattie Belle Kay Williams was the name Hattie went by. She was proud to carry her mother's name, which was Hattie Belle Latimer Kay. It is apparent that she was also proud of the Kay name because she continued to use it even after she became the wife of Bernard Williams. Kay was the family name of the white planters in South Carolina who owned Hattie's slave ancestors. Hattie's great-grandmother, Rachel, assumed the Kay name for herself and for her son Lawrence after emancipation in 1865. Three generations of the Kay family kept the slaves they owned.

Thanks to the Kay Family Association and the genealogical work they have done, Hattie's ancestry can be traced with certainty to 1790 and a man named Robert Kay. Circumstantial evidence supports that this Robert Kay was a great-grandson of James Kay, a Lancashire man who settled on the Rappahannock River in the 1660s in what is now King George County, Virginia.

When Robert Kay migrated from Virginia to upstate South Carolina in 1794, he brought with him his wife, Priscilla, his five sons, one of his two daughters, and a young slave couple, Cato and Unity, and their children. The plantation Robert Kay purchased in 1794 totaled 630 acres on Broadmouth Creek in Anderson County, South Carolina. When Robert and his wife died in 1808 the appraisal of their property included the names of this slave couple and their children.

At the estate sale of Robert and Priscilla, no mention was made that Cato and Unity were sold. Family historians Don Kay and the Reverend Jeremiah Palmer suggest that they were distributed to Robert Kay's children. They know that Cato and Unity's son, Peter, became the property of Robert's son, William. When William died, Peter became the property of William's son, Strother Kay. Hattie's great-grandmother, born in 1835, was a daughter of Peter. Strother Kay died without a will, but the appraisal of his estate listed twelve slaves, among whom were Rachel and her two younger children, John and Margaret, as worth $1,000. Rachel's son, Lawrence, Hattie's grandfather, was valued at $500. This was in 1861 and Lawrence would have been nine years old.

Strother Kay's widow, Sallie, and her white children bought back all twelve slaves. Sallie bought old Peter for $5 and paid $1,250 for Rachel and her two younger children. Sallie's son, William Pinckney, bought Lawrence for $680. The remaining slaves were bought by Sallie's other children. The white Kays paid more for the slaves than their appraised value. The reason for this is unknown but it is a fair guess that it was because there were slave traders at the sale, which drove up the prices. From the stories of the Kay family, it is my sense that the Kays felt a deep sense of loyalty to these people and their progeny who had served their family for three generations.

Rachel Kay Grave. Used by permission: Williams Family.

Of the Strother Kay slaves, only one was known to be mulatto, and that was Lawrence, Hattie's grandfather. His black mother was Rachel and his white biological father was said to be Nimrod Kay, the eldest son of Strother and a Civil War veteran. After emancipation in 1865, Rachel and Lawrence took the name Kay and stayed in the area of Neal's Creek, South Carolina, and the area of the white Kays' land.

In the 1870 census Lawrence, who was eighteen and listed as black, was living with his mother, Rachel, and Franklin, his stepfather, both slaves, and their four children. In the 1880 census, Lawrence was listed as mulatto. He was by then married to Nancy Gaillard, who was also recorded as mulatto. In that census, they had four children. In the 1900 census, they were recorded as the parents of seventeen children, twelve of them living. Among them was Hattie's father, Marion L. Kay.

Hattie's mother, Hattie Belle Latimer, was the first-born child of Wesley Latimer's second marriage. There were four children from his first marriage and ten from his second. The 1920 census says that Hattie

Belle, who was twelve, and her sister, Cornelia, who was nine, were farm laborers.

Hattie Kay Williams remembered from family stories that her mother was allowed to go to school because she was the oldest of eleven children. Therefore, she was the one who did not have to pick cotton. According to Hattie, her mother

> went to an institute called Lloyd Garrison Institute, and that was highly unusual for blacks to even finish eighth grade in those days. It was a black school because blacks didn't get to go to school except if it wasn't the season for picking cotton and you had to be in the field to work. In other offseasons, then you might be able to go to school some. My mother was sent off to this Garrison Institute, and so she was a better-educated girl.
>
> …She got to go off to this school so she was quite—you know—the lady. And Aunt Emma in Chicago was working for white folks. She sent her nice cast-off clothing which was better than the muslin that the other girls were wearing. So that's my mother. I never knew her to misspell a word. She could read and write very well.[2]

Marion L. Kay and Hattie Belle Latimer were both born in Anderson County and grew up there on neighboring plantations. Don Kay, genealogist of the white Kay family, wrote that there were "a goodly number of intermarriages between white Kays and white Latimers and perhaps their slaves as well. I grew up in Belton with many of Lawrence Kay's descendants, and there were a lot of black Latimers, some with a slight difference in spelling. The fact that Hattie Kay's parents were from those two families is not surprising."[3]

Hattie said that she and her siblings always wondered at the difference in the looks of their parents.

---

2 Olin Eugene Myers (student at the University of Chicago, currently Professor at Huxley College of the Environment at Western Washington University in Bellingham, Washington), in discussion with Hattie Bell Williams, June 1986, 18.
3 Don Kay, email message to author, August 3, 2017.

> We asked a lot of questions because there was such a difference in the looks of my Dad and the looks of my Mother. My mother was a very dignified black woman, but a jet—I wouldn't say jet black, but very, very dark complexion. Black woman. My father was very fair and he did not look right to us. We wondered, well now wait a minute. How come you're this color and then—my mother... He wasn't a mulatto—his father was a mulatto.[4]

The 1920 census records that Marion Kay and Hattie Belle Latimer were married in Chicago on June 30, 1917 and lived on South Lake Park Avenue in Hyde Park. At that time, the area was mixed income and racially diverse with blacks being the minority.

During the late nineteenth century, Chicago's most prestigious residential street was Prairie Avenue, a north-south street on the South Side. Powerful people such as Marshall Field, founder of the dry goods store that made State Street famous; George Pullman, designer of the railroad car that bears his name; W. W. Kimball, maker of pianos and organs; and Philip Armour, a meatpacking industrialist, lived on this avenue in grand mansions. Today Chicago's most famous area of wealthy people is the Gold Coast, which is just north of the Loop, but the area on Prairie Avenue predated it and was called "Millionaire's Row." The mansions clustered there belonged to the men who made Chicago a global city. Not only were the owners of the mansions famous, so were the architects who designed them.

By the time Hattie's parents moved to Chicago in 1917, the mansions were being abandoned as their wealthy owners fled to the Gold Coast in reaction to the rapidly increasing number of blacks migrating to Chicago from the South. Fine old homes were divided into as many small apartments as possible. Each apartment of two or three rooms was outfitted with a small kitchen. They could hardly be called "apartments," so they became known simply as "kitchenettes." Hattie's family lived in a building a few blocks east of Millionaire's Row, which was built to be an apartment building.

When Hattie was born in 1922, the Kays had three children: Lawrence, who was three, Alberta, who was one, and Marion, who was under a year

---
4 Myers, interview, 18.

old. Another son, Alvin, was born after Marion but died on December 13, 1921, at the age of nine months. A year later, on December 7, 1922, Hattie and her twin sister, Mattie, were born at home. Soon after their birth, the baby girls developed pneumonia. Their mother, with the help and advice of a neighbor woman who was German, worked to treat the babies. Hattie's mother told her about the struggle to keep the girls alive.

> A German neighbor came over with this poultice, something from the Old Country with red onions and goose grease and all this crap. She put it on my chest and back, and she sat with me during the night with this newspaper over a kettle, you know, to steam me out. And she told me never to forget, if it hadn't been for this white German woman, I wouldn't even be alive. She told me at that time because I had been going through some things in school and she set me aright.[5]

Hattie survived but Mattie died when she was thirteen days old. Mrs. Kay told the story of the German woman to Hattie and her other children as a way of teaching them that there are good, caring people in the white race who can be trusted. In spite of their grief over the loss of Alvin and Mattie, Hattie Belle and Marion had five more children: Edwin, Jerome, Richard, Julia, and Azella.

The Dixie Melody Masters, Program Brochure, undated, 4. Used by permission: The University of Iowa Libraries, Iowa Digital Library.

Hattie's father was a singer, with a dramatic tenor voice. (This is the most common of the tenors and regarded as the mainstay of the tenor family, being a good all-around voice with considerable projection.) For fifteen years, Marion toured the United States and Canada as a member of the Dixie Melody Masters, sending money home from his engagements to support his family. Other members of the quartet were not so faithful about that. This caused Mrs. Kay some distress when the other quartet wives found out that she received support from her traveling husband, but they did not.

---

5 Myers, interview, 49.

A stop on one of Marion's tours was mentioned in a high school newspaper in Ogden, Utah, on April 5, 1938, reporting that the Dixie Melody Masters were going to perform at an assembly in the Weber High School auditorium. The article stated that the quartet would "present famous spirituals, tunes of the South, plantation melodies, camp meeting songs, and slavery day songs."[6]

Another performance was in Collegeville, Minnesota, on December 10, 1936, at St. John's University. The school's newspaper reported that the members of the quartet were "accomplished singers individually, and each has had experience on both the concert stage and in radio." They sang a variety of Southern songs and their own arrangements of popular favorites.[7]

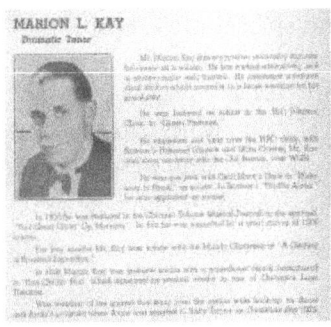

Marion L. Kay, The Dixie Melody Masters, Program Brochure, undated, 2. Used by permission: The University of Iowa Libraries, Iowa Digital Library.

Marion Kay was a soloist with the Cecil Mack Choir in the Broadway production of *Rhapsody in Black* at the Sam Harris Theatre in New York City in 1931. Ethel Waters was the star of the show, which ran for eighty performances. Marion's career in music included singing, as a featured soloist, with the Hall Johnson Choir in the movie version of *Green Pastures*.

Music was Marion's passion, but none of his performances paid enough to support a family of eleven so he worked in the Chicago stockyards and in the steel mills. The 1930 census listed him as a laborer. In 1938, it was reported that he made $250 for the year for his performances. The 1940 census listed his occupation as singer.

The 1930 census reports that the family was living in Manhattan, New York City, on West 123rd Street between Seventh and Eighth Avenues. Their home would have been near the Apollo Theater. It is the most famous

---

6   Helen Rouse, "Negro Artists to be Heard," *The Ogden Standard-Examiner*, April 5, 1938, 10, https://www.newspapers.com/image/?spot=7888934&fcfToken=746c2b454e505158547764374 86948474a4f365063426e3250694e58337a34765275454b6f71756f586c6d592b586f796935612b3 8363438724a5a646c526571.

7   "Dixie Melody Masters to Entertain Sunday," *St John's Record* (Collegeville, MN), December 6, 1936, 1, http://cdm.csbsju.edu/digital/collection/CSBArchNews/id/28333.

performance venue associated with African American entertainers and is now a historic landmark. World famous musicians such as Louis Armstrong, Bill "Bojangles" Robinson, and Ella Fitzgerald performed there. The family's move to New York City probably had much to do with opportunities for Marion on the musical scene. Sadly, however, the census report in its planned brevity reveals only that Marion was a laborer in the "ice industry" and Hattie Belle was a janitress in the "house industry." The family lived in New York City for two years.

Returning to Chicago, the Kay family of eleven moved into a first floor, six-room apartment at 5216 South Lake Park. Across the street was the Robinson Coal Yard, a police station, and the Illinois Central Railroad. This railroad became a migrant trail, bringing hundreds of thousands of blacks to Chicago from the South over several decades. The Kay apartment was a cold water flat with three sources for heat: an oil stove in the living room, a coal stove in the kitchen, and a gas stove in the kitchen on which Hattie Belle cooked for her family.

Hattie recalled that her parents were very hard-working people but still could not afford proper clothes for all their children. From time to time, Hattie and her siblings received clothing from a "clothing wardrobe" at Kenwood School, which at that time was integrated with very few black students. Few other students in the school needed clothing because they were the children of wealthy Jewish people who were the majority at that time. Hattie's mother would send a note to Mrs. Greenberg saying, "Well, Hattie will not be able to come to school until I can get her some shoes."

> There was a little clothing wardrobe woman, a Jewish woman named Mrs. Greenberg, and she had this little room at Kenwood with an ironing board, and clothes on hangers, shoes and socks, and Mrs. Greenberg would call me to come down to the clothing room. Fifteen minutes before final dismissal bell she would have this bundle of blouses and sweaters and things ready for me, and she would have shoes for me, I remember those little black patent leather shoes, they reminded me of that little song, "Shoes to Set My Feet A-Dancing."

And I was dancing down the park. They weren't new, but she polished them, she put new shoe strings in them, all this meticulous care, and you know what I said then? "When I get big, I'm going to help people like this." I have done it and I'll be darned if I haven't maintained the clothing wardrobe all these years. Where do I get it from? The adults who impressed me when I was a little kid.[8]

Later in the interview, Hattie said she was so embarrassed that she didn't want any of her schoolmates to see her wearing clothes from the second-hand clothes closet. Hattie described her parents with these words:

My father never drove. He just rode public transportation. He was a hard-working father, a man. His hobbies were his music, fishing when he could get time. Sometimes over by the lake. He was a gentleman. And so we had a loving mother. She took in laundry. And we made ends meet and we never knew hunger. We didn't have much. Mom would make those big biscuits or cornbread or some beans or whatnot, but we said a blessing before we ate. We were in a school system where we could compete and had to learn. And that was good. Coming up that way, the thing I remember is that I never got anything new. It was always hand-me-down things, and I was midway, sort of and never got to do things. The older kids always got new things, and they were handed down to the younger ones. And also it went that way with anything. Now, like my mom thought that my older sister, being the older girl, she should be the one to have the music lessons. Not necessarily the talented kid, but the oldest girl, the music teacher would come for 25¢ lesson and my mother would pay that and Alberta would be in the parlor at the old upright and she was never inclined to play the piano. I yearned to play the piano. I yearned and would stand at the parlor door. I would look in. I so wanted to play that piano. And I didn't know where to find middle C. And you know what? I wanted to play so bad that I would go in and tinker around at the piano when there was time, and there was always plenty of time for that. I play by ear today.[9]

---

8 Myers, interview, 14.
9 Myers, interview, 10.

That much I remember, but I also remember my parents were very, very strict. Too strict. In fact, when we were growing up, my brothers had complete freedom. It was a kind of family where you waited on your brothers. If they wanted water at the table, you waited on the men folks. My kind of house was that the girls fixed the beds and did all the housework. The boys did not have to wash dishes. Now they had jobs after school. They were shoeshine boys working on the paper newsstands, things like that, but they had no housework or anything to do, and they had the freedom to…If they were out at work, and they were going to go out to the beach or they could go roller skating or to a dance. But the girls were almost kept in a sheltered kind of the situation. We weren't allowed to go to the beach. My mother felt that was like showing your body in a public bathtub, that was her words. Her daughters would not be in a public situation with their bodies uncovered.[10]

The Kay home was in Hyde Park, which had a majority white population. Hattie's sister, Julia Liddell, tells the story that when Hattie was a teenager she would take her little sisters, Julia and Azella, to the whites-only kiddie pool at East End Park, which was just off 53rd Street toward the lake. The park was situated among big hotels inhabited by white families, some of whom had black nannies. She said that when they got in the pool all the white children either would run away or be removed by their white mothers or black nannies. "We were like flies in buttermilk." The Kay children knew they weren't wanted there, but they found some pleasure in the fact that they had the whole pool to themselves after the white kids ran away. While three-year-old Julia enjoyed having the pool all to herself and her siblings, Hattie felt high tension not only from the white people but also from the police and her mother.

> So these were innocent little kids that want to get in the water so I see no reason why they shouldn't get in the water so I put them in the water and I let them play in the water in the kiddie pool on East 53rd Street at East End Park. Well, this was a no-no, so the older black women said, "That little snippet, that little thing, there. She's going to cause trouble out here." So all young mothers would call their kids out of the water. And so then it just would be these little black kids in the water. So you could just cut through the hostility with

---

10 Myers, interview, 11.

a knife. And pretty soon, the Chicago police department was located right at 53rd and Lake Park—that was a police station. So they came across the street and they said to my mother, "Mrs. Kay, your daughter's causing problems over at the kiddie pool at East End Park. See that she keeps the kids out of the water—just for the peace in the neighborhood, have her to not let the kids get in the water." So then again, my mom called me aside and said, "now you can't let the kids wade in the water over there. Now if you walk around the park, don't let them get in the water."[11]

So I disobeyed her. I didn't intend to disobey her, but I had let my three-year-old sister in the water so many times, how are you going to walk by on a hot summer day and say, "No. Now you can't get in." So Azella just had a fit and being only three and a cute little chubby doll, she just ran and plunged in the water. Well the mothers called every one of the children out, they would do this. "Larry!" And this little kid's name was Larry, and so he screamed and hollered because he was a little kid, about three. He didn't know why all of a sudden he had to come out of the water. So he had a real fit that day and all the kids, they didn't want to come out, because the kids didn't understand. They were innocent. But Azella, my three-year-old sister, going over with her little shovel and her bucket, to offer it to this little white kid, name Larry because he cried! She was trying to console him. And he shut up, and between the two of them, by some means, two innocent children solve this situation that could have been a dynamite situation. It came to the point where the pool was integrated by the Kay family.[12]

Julia's memories of her sister also include her claim that Hattie may have been the first black person to integrate a lunch counter. This was in the early 1930s. Their mother would give Hattie money to buy ice cream at Walgreens drug store for herself and the younger children. It was permitted for black people to buy food and drink at the lunch counter, but not to sit there. Hattie would buy the ice cream and then instruct the

---

11 Myers, interview, 14.
12 Myers, interview, 51.

children to sit down at the counter. Julia says they were never asked to leave. She thinks it may have been because they were just cute little girls.

Hattie and her siblings went to school at the Kenwood Elementary School. When she graduated from Kenwood, Hattie wrote this song and the class sang it on the day of their graduation:

> *Dear Kenwood School,*
> *You've crowned our hopes this graduation day.*
> *Our love for you*
> *So pure and true will never fade away.*
> *We've struggled hard*
> *And struggled long to reach this shining goal.*
>
> *Our day has come.*
> *We've reached success.*
> *Our diplomas now we hold.*
> *Goodbye to you Kenwood.*
> *We will remember your name,*
> *For you've led us onward*
> *To the paths of fame.*
>
> *Onward ever onward*
> *Into the world we'll go.*
> *For you've made us happy*
> *With our hearts all aglow.*
> *Goodbye to you Kenwood.*
> *We will conquer all.*
>
> *Dearest Alma Mater*
> *Though we bid you ado*
> *We will remember your banner*
> *And be grateful to you.*
> *We will work for honor*
> *And look up to your name*

For you've left us happy.
Honor is our aim.
Goodbye to Kenwood.
We will cherish your name.

The memories of this song were bittersweet for Hattie even into her later years. She was proud to have her song chosen and sung, but she was very disappointed that the teacher added another line written by a white classmate of hers. Hattie said it went against the grain of the teacher to admit that a black student was the author of these words sung to the tune of "Pomp and Circumstance." By adding another line, the teacher was able to attribute it to Hattie Williams and Barbara Unger. They sang those words at every Kenwood graduation for the next twenty years with it being attributed to the Class of 1937.

Hattie enjoyed reading but her mother would not let her borrow books from the library for fear the little kids might tear up the books and she wouldn't have the money to pay for them. So, Hattie spent hours reading and studying in the Blackstone Library. In addition, she had some opportunities with school assignments. She tells of reading books and giving reports on them. Her favorite book was *Up from Slavery* by Booker T. Washington.

> He was interested in education, but I remember my judgment of him. At that time, and I find that I think like him now, but when I was a kid, I thought he was an "Uncle Tom," because I read a passage in the book, where he was teaching good grooming, and he had formed his educational institution. He had told the young people that they had to have a toothbrush, and he went to the girls' dormitory, and he wanted to see if everyone had their toothbrush, their comb, and other grooming things. And so, all four girls held up one toothbrush, and said, "Oh, we got ours." And I was offended because I was in an all-white school, and this was required reading, and all I could read out of this is a derogatory statement that blacks all use the same toothbrush. It was out of context, see? But in later years, I have stood accused of being an "Uncle Tom," myself. "She got all these white folks living in her house, she got all these white folks around her, and she is an 'Uncle Tom.'" They're only here to

study, they're only here to get something done…When he was writing *Up from Slavery*, well, that book as I see it now, it showed the struggle that he had to go through, even to get the funds from whites, to have the school. He was fighting for his people. I didn't see it as a child. So that was one book that made an impression on me.[13]

Hattie in 1940. Used by permission: Williams Family.

The 1940 census reports that Hattie was living in New York City again. This time she was staying with her Aunt Elsie and her maternal grandparents, Elizabeth and Preston Latimer, at 261 West 129th Place. At this point in her life, she had completed the eighth grade. After her sophomore year, she dropped out of school to help support her family. Eventually, she earned her GED.

In 1948, when the favorite teacher of the Kay children retired, Hattie was twenty-six. Her little sister, Julia, asked Hattie to write a poem for Mrs. Wayser's retirement.

The teacher dearest to my heart
From Kenwood School must now depart.
With hair of silver and heart of gold
Though some may feel she is growing old,
I know that time can never wear her spirit
For there is music there.

In history class she might be stern
And make me know that I must learn.
And yet when music class would start
She taught me music from her heart.
As long as Kenwood stands here
I won't forget Mrs. Wayser dear.
Although her teaching days are done
Her pupils loved her everyone.

---

13 Myers, interview, 47.

Kenwood School at that time was a white school with a sprinkling of black students. Hattie's brother, Richard, is the only black child in his 1948 graduating class picture. The push to remove blacks from the Hyde Park-Kenwood area, which abutted the Black Belt to the south, began in earnest during Hattie's childhood and adolescence. All around her, the neighborhood underwent drastic changes through what was called "urban renewal."

A study done by sociologists Otis Dudley Duncan and Beverly Duncan in 1950 analyzed 175 census tracts in Chicago and classified them in terms of stages of racial transition.[14] They classified most of Oakland, where Hattie owned her home, as an "invasion" area from 1940-1950. The inference was that blacks were coming to Chicago in overpowering numbers like an invading army. War metaphors describing this movement of people were common. One analysis said that when physical barriers such as a railway or any area that previously separated white from black are overcome that is the first event of the invasion process. Hattie's family was hardly made up of invaders. They had been residents of the area since 1917.

Hattie's Family, Top Row: Brian, Bruce, Bradford, Bernard Jr.; Bottom Row: Briscoe, Hattie, Bernard Sr., Barbara. Used by permission: Williams Family.

In 1943, Hattie married Alonzo Mead and their daughter Barbara was born. They were divorced and she married Bernard Williams in 1945. Bernard and Hattie first rented one room in the fifteen-room house at 4064 South Lake Park for ten dollars a week. Later they bought the house. Bernard's entire career was at the Post Office, where many African Americans found steady jobs. By the time he worked there the discriminatory practices that had prevailed in the postal system before 1940 were replaced by an atmosphere that encouraged equal treatment and opportunities for advancement. He died in 1979. Hattie raised their children at 4064 South Lake Park and lived the rest of her life in the three-story Vic-

---

14 Otis Dudley Duncan and Beverly Duncan, *The Negro Population of Chicago: A Study of Residential Succession* (Chicago: University of Chicago, 1957), quoted in Mary Pattillo, *Black on the Block: The Politics of Race and Class in the City* (Chicago: University of Chicago Press, 2007), 45.

torian house, with the exception of some months in a retirement home shortly before she died.

In the years between 1946 and 1951, Hattie gave birth to four of her five sons: Bernard, Brian, Bruce, and Bradford. Her fifth son, Briscoe, was born in 1953. Her small children, Barbara and Bernard, were now in school for only half days because the schools were overcrowded. Bruce and Briscoe would soon follow their siblings into a less than adequate school situation at Oakenwald Elementary School across the street from their home. Racial hatred, blatantly expressed and violently acted out, swirled around Hattie and her family throughout her childbearing years.

In 1951 Hattie became the first black president of the Parent Teacher Association at Oakenwald School. Hattie's son, Bernard, said:

> There were less than twenty black families living in the area then. The school was segregated and students attended classes in shifts. White students were in class in the morning and black, Hispanic and Asian in the afternoon. She became alarmed at the lack of resources and books with pages torn out that the minority grade schoolers had to endure and protested to the school principal. She coldly advised Hattie to stay in her place and not to make an issue of the matter as blacks were relegated to remedial instruction due to their lack of native intelligence. I recall my mother's infuriation [sic] after that meeting with the principal and her resolve to raise money for better books and supplies through bake sales. Which she did with amazing success.[15]

The 1950s and 1960s were a golden time for Hattie's neighborhood, which by then had become predominately black. There were stores for shopping, theatres, and a bowling alley. However, the prize of the neighborhood was the Sutherland Hotel. Musicians such as Thelonious Monk, Max Roach, and Miles Davis (and his sidemen John Coltrane and Cannonball Adderley) all played at the Sutherland Lounge, which was located at 47th and Drexel, a few blocks

Hattie in 1949. Used by permission: Williams Family.

---

15 Bernard Williams Jr., unpublished letter, 2011. This was the letter from Hattie's son to the Park District Board of Directors. See page 130.

from Hattie's home. The lounge was called "black and tan" because white and black people together enjoyed its entertainment. Clubs such as these were a horror to whites who dreaded racial commingling.

High rise tenements loom as "concentration camps of public housing" says Hattie Williams. This work is licensed under the Creative Commons Attribution ShareAlike 4.0 License.

In 1951, the first high-rise building of the Lake Front Properties public housing was built across the street from Hattie's home. Hattie had been surrounded by poverty before but the "stockpiling" of black families in public housing intensified the culture of poverty. Before 1962, four more high-rises were built on that site. These buildings made a half-mile wall of public housing where before there had been individual family homes. One hundred and fifty families moved into the first building, swelling the population of the Oakenwald Elementary School where Hattie's children were pupils and Hattie was president of the PTA.

Traditionally PTA groups organize activities to support school programs and do fundraising for their individual school. Hattie worked with the members of her PTA to accomplish such goals, but she went beyond that. One of the things Hattie did as PTA president was to bring voting machines into the black schools so the students could experience what it was like to vote. She described this action.

> One of the things that I felt inspired to do as the PTA president during the civil rights movement was to bring the voting machines into the black schools. That we could have student council elections, and really inform the young people in a way that they would know how to split a vote, write in a candidate, and all of this. So I did fundraising and the PTA, you know bake sales and a sock hop dance or something, and we paid for the cartage of these heavy voting machines that were in use during the civil rights movement.

> The big gray upright machines, and we brought them into the schools. I got away with that for a couple of years, but then, this is too much voter education to the students. I knew that there would be 18-year-olds allowed to vote in later years. But what happened is, the Chicago Board of Elections said, "we cannot have you use the machines anymore."[16]

Hattie went to one of the aldermen in another ward whom she thought would be sympathetic and supportive of the voting machines in the black schools. He refused to help her. Hattie said, "I see these machines are still in use in the white schools. That's where I got the idea. It's not a new idea. It's only new among blacks."[17]

Her first presidency of the PTA at Oakenwald School led to her becoming president of the PTA at Forestville North's Upper Grade Center, and by the 1960s, she was president of the Southeast Council of PTAs which covered more than forty schools. Two years after Hattie became the PTA president, Benjamin C. Willis became superintendent of the Chicago Public Schools. He denied any racist intentions in the locations of schools which kept them segregated. He attributed the poor quality of education in black schools as due only to overcrowding. His arrival on the scene was the beginning of a period of activism in Hattie's life. She was at the center of protests and boycotts until Willis retired in 1966.

In 1966, she was given a Life Membership in the Illinois Congress of PTAs; "This honor acknowledges that the recipient has given meritorious and dedicated service to the welfare of children and youth."[18]

Hattie's dedication to young people was also recognized by two other important awards. The Eleanor Roosevelt Foundation Award for Outstanding Service to Youth was given to her in 1964. This award brought with it a check for $800 which Hattie used to start the Oakland Learning Center, a storefront learning center for children in the neighborhood. Franklin D. Roosevelt III came to Chicago to present the check to her.[19] The learning center was destroyed in a fire set by an arsonist. Hattie's strong belief was that the destruction of her learning center was a political action.

---

16 Myers, interview, 38.
17 Myers, interview, 38.
18 https://illinoispta.org/
19 "That They Might Learn," *Ebony* 20, no. 5 (March 1965): 93-8.

The Chicago Urban League was the trustee of the money. Edwin C. Berry, executive director of the Urban League at the time, described Hattie with these words:

> Mrs. Williams is very talented in involving other adults in the community and has developed a group of parents who are central to the operation of the study center... she is exactly the type of person who deserves support... as a community leader dealing with educational problems both in her community and in Chicago.[20]

The state of Illinois honored her work on behalf of youth by awarding her the State of Illinois Citation Award for Outstanding Service to Youth in 1965.

Hattie was a strong woman who gave of herself to her family, friends, and church in every way she could. That strength became brightly manifest and public as she suffered from brain tumors. In 1966, she had the first of three brain tumor surgeries. She described her condition: "When I was hospitalized under my afflictions, I lost my speech and was completely paralyzed. I made a vow with the Lord that if I survived I would serve my fellow man."[21] At this time, Hattie had five sons and a daughter between the ages of thirteen and twenty-two. Along with the vow to serve people, she longed to survive in order to protect her children from the dangers ever present in the neighborhood.

After her recovery from the first surgery, in keeping with her promise to serve people, she began organizing prayer groups among women on welfare. She spoke and preached in white churches throughout the Chicago area, telling them of the desperate need of people in the ghetto for basics such as food, clothes, laundry soap, and toilet paper. She began to ask for donations and discovered that she had a knack for moving people to become involved. As she did with all good things, she attributed her success to God. "The Lord gave me a sixth sense, a kind of instinct to know how far to go and when to go," she explained.[22]

---

20 Memorandum from Orin Lehman to the Trustees of the Eleanor Roosevelt Memorial Foundation, RE Eleanor Roosevelt Awards submitted by Harold Taylor and approved by the Trustee Sub-Committee on Awards, July 7, 1964.
21 W. Halamandaris, "Hattie Kay Williams," *Caring* (1988): 34.
22 Halamandaris, "Hattie Kay Williams," 34.

From 1967-1969 she served as a school representative on the Human Relations Department of the Chicago Board of Education. In 1973, she ran for the office of alderman for the Fourth Ward, which included her neighborhood. Her opponent was Timothy C. Evans, who became the Chief Judge of the Cook County Circuit Court, the first black Chief Judge of this court. Hattie's goals and those of Evans were the same—improve life for everyone in Bronzeville. After the election, she continued steadfastly to provide services that were sadly lacking in the neighborhood. Alderman Evans supported her in these events and attended many of them.

Hattie's ministry took on a more formal shape in 1978 when she and Claude Marie Barbour joined together to form a Shalom Community in her home. Hattie discovered that Claude Marie had the same idea about "mission-in-reverse"[23] and had put the vision into practice when she was a pastor in Gary, Indiana.

Hattie and Claude Marie called it mission-in-reverse because their vision was that people who came to the ghetto to "do mission" among the residents there would learn from the residents. Too often people came from outside with their own plan for what they would do for the people. Hattie and Claude Marie wanted those people to come and to learn from the people. Hattie referred to the residents as the "teachers" and the visitors as the "reachers."

Together the two women established Hattie's home as a place from which students from the Catholic Theological Union and nearby religious orders could work with Hattie and others in the neighborhood. Some eventually would even live for a time in Hattie's home (men's community) or in a nearby apartment (women's community) so that they could get to know and understand people in the neighborhood in a deeper way.

---

23 Claude Marie described mission-in-reverse this way: "We believe that as ministers and missionaries, we can and should learn from the people we serve—especially from the poor and marginalized. When ministry is grounded in mutuality and solidarity, ministers become persons immersed in the world of others, like Jesus was in the world of His time. A minister's mission emerges in dialogue with others and is given definite direction as the result of this mutuality." Stephen Bevans, SVD, Eleanor Doidge, LoB, and Robert Schreiter, CPPS, *The Healing Circle: Essays in Cross-Cultural Mission Presented to the Rev. Dr. Claude Marie Barbour* (Chicago: CCGM Publications, 2000), 201.

Hattie was further honored in her life-time by a receiving a Black Liberation Award, hosted in June 1975 from Kuumba, Chicago's long-time black theatre group. Though focusing on "Black Theater," Kuumba nevertheless encompassed "the total cultural spectrum." In a *Black World* notice of this event, it lists Hattie as a "beloved community activist" and Girl Scout official.[24]

Black Liberation Awards, May 18, 1974. *Sun-Times*. Photo credit: Bob Black. Used by permission: *Chicago Sun-Times*.

In 1983, Hattie received an honorary doctorate from Anna Marie College in Paxton, Massachusetts. A description of the degree states that it is not awarded based on research done by the recipient and that the College gives other degrees for achievement in science, government, and religion. Hattie K. Williams's doctorate is a Doctorate of Humane Letters conferred on Hattie to honor her contributions to society.[25]

Hattie continued to serve God and the people in her neighborhood through the 1980s even though her health was failing. She underwent surgery for a brain tumor in 1981 and again in 1987. After the latter procedure, she declared she would never have another surgery. Her doctors concurred in that decision.

Hattie Receiving Doctor of Humane Letters from Anna Marie College, Paxton, MA, 1983. Used by permission: Williams Family.

In 1989, she was given an award by the Caring Institute which each year awards four or five Americans "for acts of caring and "humanitarian services around the country and internationally." The Caring Institute website with Hattie's award entry, lists the wrong year for her award, but lists numerous works and programs, especially Shalom Community as reasons she was inducted into

---

24 "Kuumba's 1975 Black Liberation Awards," *Black World* 24, no. 10 (April 1976): 72.
25 Anna Marie College, Paxton, MA, Doctor of Humane Letters, 1983.

the prestigious group.²⁶ She died on August 31, 1990, in her home in the Lake Meadows Apartments.

Hattie at Caring Awards with Daughter Barbara and Sister Julia Liddell, and Hattie's Friends, 1988. Used by permission: Caring Institute, Washington, DC.

---

26 "Hattie Williams," The Caring Institute, 2019, https://www.caring.org/.

Chapter 3
RACE RIOT

When Hattie was growing up in Hyde Park, the main inhabitants were white, even though there was a black ghetto just north of her family's home. The censuses of 1910 and 1920 report that Hyde Park was 2 percent to 5 percent black. Hattie attended school in Hyde Park when it was not easy to be black in the district, but her wise parents taught her much about race relations.

Hattie said in an interview:

> But as a child you go through stages. I remember I went through a phase where I hated all white people. I guess I did because I was the only black in my class, and of course I suffered some insults and whatnot, but the reason I went through this is, I must have been about thirteen years old and in the seventh or eighth grade. I remember we did book reports; very thorough book reports, and the book that we had to read was *Uncle Tom's Cabin* by Harriet Beecher Stowe. As you read about Uncle Tom and Simon Legree and he was always hitting niggers upside the head and all, this infuriated me to have to stand up and read this in class with all white students.
>
> Also, I began to get emotionally overrun by this. I was walking down Lake Park going home from school and I was wondering, "Well, why did God make me like this?" Looking at my brown arms. I had a teacher who must have been very sensitive, because she said, "Now, children, we are going to study the life of Harriet Beecher Stowe and why this book was written." Being a very wise teacher—I can look back at that and see it now, although I didn't see it then—that this was a preparation for me. When I studied the life of Harriet Beecher Stowe and found out that this woman was actually a very sensitive white woman, writing vignettes, which I am

> attempting to do now, in a white abolitionist newspaper, and I said, "How could I hate white people when this woman was sensitive enough to write about this problem in such a way?"
>
> My mother and father were southern immigrants from South Carolina. My mother would always say, "Well, you know, we got to always stay in our place." I wanted to say, "What is my place?" I was angry, I had anger. My mother said, "Look, young lady, you owe your very life to that German neighbor of mine who came over to this coal-heated house that was real cold, and you and your twin both caught pneumonia. Two seven-pound twins caught pneumonia, and Mattie died. You wouldn't have lived if this German neighbor hadn't come over. I was young then, and she knew how to put poultices of onions and goose-grease on you, and she knew how to make a little tent of newspaper, and she brought you through the crisis. So get it through your head that people are people."[27]

Hattie learned another lesson about white people from her Dad when he told her about the race riot that threatened their family in 1919, three years before she was born.

> One time I came home from school with some story, and I was upset, and I wanted him to come to school to see about me. My dad sat me down and told me about 1919 after World War I. There was a big immigration of blacks from the South to Chicago. They would take jobs in the meat processing plants at a cheaper wage than the Italians, Lithuanians, Polish, and other people and it brought about attention, and there was a big race riot.
>
> There were cobblestone streets, horses and buggies on the streets in those days in 1919. He said he got up and went to work, he didn't realize there was any trouble. But when he got there this Polish fellow said, "Hey, what'd you come here for? Don't you know there's trouble?" and he puts my dad in a buggy, whipped up the horses, and covered my dad with a

---

27 Hattie Williams, interview with Betsy Edwards, August 3, 1988, 7.

blanket, brought him all the way back to Hyde Park where we lived, and said, "Look, you just stay in the house, and we'll see about you and your kids until this mess rolls over."

So he said that a Polish man helped him to get out of a situation where it could have meant his death. We were on a white island in Hyde Park, and being brought food and whatnot and sheltered through a race riot. So with that, they taught me that people are people, and when you have that kind of background, you can look back on it and say that even then the Lord was preparing me for a cross-cultural kind of work. Because of this I have always viewed people as individuals, not as "blacks" or "whites" and this has been helpful to me.[28]

The Chicago race riot of 1919 was part of an explosion of violence between white and black people in over two dozen cities across the country. There was so much violence and bloodshed that the summer was called "the Red Summer of 1919." Even though Hattie wasn't born at the time of this riot, it had a lasting effect on her life.

The riot in Chicago started on Sunday, July 27, and lasted until Saturday, August 2. Before the riot was over, 15 whites and 23 blacks were dead and 195 whites and 342 blacks injured. Hattie's father could easily have been killed or injured as he made his way to his job in the stockyards. Black people who worked in the stockyards had to walk through white areas to get to and from work, which left them unprotected from white men and boys who banded together in mobs to attack them.

One thousand people were left homeless after arson fires destroyed their homes. The combination of prolonged arson, looting, and murder made this the worst rioting in Illinois history. The riot started at the 29th Street Beach on Lake Michigan where some black adults who wanted to use the beach met resistance from whites. It was a tense situation at that location but what set off the riot was the drowning of Eugene Williams, a seventeen-year-old black teenager, at the 25th Street Beach.

Eugene and three friends had a favorite spot on the beach where they kept a fourteen- by nine-foot raft they had made with several other teenagers. They called the area "the hot and the cold" because the hot water

---

28 Edwards, interview, 8.

from a brewery and the cold water from an ice company flowed together at this spot. None of the boys could swim well, but their fun was cooling off in the water by diving from the raft, paddling, and returning to the raft to dive in again. As often as they could during the summer, they went to this beach and floated out into Lake Michigan while always being careful to avoid an imaginary line that separated the "whites only" section from the "blacks only" section. On July 27, 1919, a Sunday afternoon, Eugene was in the water when a white man on the shore began throwing rocks at the boys. Eugene dived off the raft and was distracted by the actions of the man on the beach. At first, the boys thought it was a game, but when one of the rocks hit Eugene in the forehead he sank out of sight. One of his friends jumped in to help him but couldn't save him.

The boys reported the drowning to a white police officer who was on the beach. He refused to arrest the man who had thrown the rocks and instead arrested a black man on the complaint of some minor offense. Word of the drowning spread quickly to the already tense situation at the 29th Street Beach. Blacks mobbed the policemen and gunfire broke out between the police and blacks. By nightfall, white and black mobs were fighting each other in many areas across the city.

Unfortunately, a threatened strike by streetcar and elevated train workers on Monday morning brought a mass of makeshift vehicles clogging the streets. Many people were forced to walk to their workplaces, which in turn provided opportunities for acts of violence to be committed against them. When the workday was over, white men and boys who lived between the stockyards, where many blacks worked, and the Black Belt, where blacks lived, banded together as mobs to attack the blacks walking home. Black mobs retaliated against the white violence.

As the violence increased the police fired into a crowd of black demonstrators, killing four of them. Gangs in white areas were emboldened by this shooting. "Automobile raids were added to the rioting on Monday night. Cars from which rifle and revolver shots were fired were driven at great speed through sections inhabited by Negroes."[29] Blacks began sniping in retaliation. Faced with an undermanned police force, Mayor William H. Thompson requested the governor, Frank Lowden, to mobilize the state militia and send them to Chicago. The 3,500 men that Lowden

---

29 William M. Tuttle, *Race Riot: Chicago in the Red Summer of 1919* (New York: Atheneum, 1972), 34.

sent were housed in armories. However, the governor refused to send them out until the mayor requested that he deploy them.

On Tuesday gang violence grew worse as the strike by the streetcar workers took effect. Black workers were forced to walk to their jobs. Rumors about black attacks on whites circulated, and black mobs retaliated against violent whites. There were also sporadic violent attacks in other areas of the city, including the Chicago Loop and the West and North Sides.

By Wednesday 6,200 troops had moved into the area between 18th and 55th Streets. Lowden stated that the militia was ready, but that the mayor needed to request that they be deployed. The mayor replied that the governor didn't need his permission, but upon receiving a statement from black ministers, social workers, and professional and business leaders the mayor finally asked for the aid of the militia. There was widespread fear of a plot to burn the whole Black Belt. White mobs set the homes of black families on fire. At the time, blacks were blamed for fires that burned homes of white immigrants, but later a grand jury suspected that they were started by Back of the Yards[30] white gangs. Shortly before 10 p.m. that evening 6,200 troops were moved out of the armories into the region bounded by Wentworth and Indiana, and by 18th and 55th Streets. It was reported that the soldiers acted professionally and responded similarly regardless of whether the rioters were white or black.

On July 31, more than thirty fires were started by white rioters in the Black Belt before noon. The rioters had placed steel cables across the streets so fire trucks could not get to the fires. The mayor's office received word of a plan to burn down the black area and run its residents out of town. Between the soldiers and heavy rain, the worst of the riot ended on August 3. It was the end of the riot as such, but violence continued.

The riot did not happen solely because of the death of Eugene Williams. It was a manifestation of racial hatred and prejudice. It was the fruit of the denial to blacks of equal opportunities in employment, housing, and political power. There was a feeling among whites in Chicago that their

---

30 Back of the Yards was a neighborhood located on the south-west edge of the Union Stockyards just outside the boundaries of Chicago. The area was largely populated by thousands of Eastern European immigrants who worked in the stockyards and the nearby meatpacking plants. Upton Sinclair's 1906 novel *The Jungle* describes life in this area. Robert Frost wrote a poem about the neighborhood and gave Chicago the famous nickname "Hog Butcher for the World."

city was being overrun by black people. Between 1917 and 1919 more than 50,000 black people moved into Chicago. Where all these newcomers were permitted to live was limited by the boundaries already set as the Black Belt. It is not surprising that this caused major problems not only in housing and employment but also in the use of public spaces such as beaches and parks.

This massive move referred to by historians as the Great Migration, seriously affected the white community in the arena of employment opportunities. The influx of blacks made available a supply of workers who were used to low wages and not accustomed to labor unions. People in the white immigrant communities near the stockyards and factories were afraid of losing their jobs because blacks would work for lower wages. The unions refused to accept blacks into their membership because of their race and because they were often used by factory and company owners as strikebreakers.

As Hattie heard the story years afterward, the race riot was a major factor in the formation of her values. Even though Hattie was born three years after the riot and heard the story years afterward, her father taught her that even in the throes of murder and mayhem there were white people who would help black people. While teaching her this valuable lesson he was also teaching her about the hatred and violence that threatened black people in Chicago. Even as he brought this important lesson out of a horrifying situation, he was making her aware of how dangerous life was for black people in Chicago.

Both her mother's recounting of the help and compassion that a white woman provided at the time of life-threatening illness for her babies and her father's story of protection by a white man taught Hattie that people are people regardless of the color of their skin. She learned that neither race has a monopoly on kindness or goodness.

Chapter 4
BRONZEVILLE/OAKLAND

The name of Hattie's immediate neighborhood appears on a map of Chicago as Oakland. The wider area surrounding it, which includes North Kenwood, was dubbed the Black Belt at the beginning of the twentieth century. In 1934 the black residents of the area proudly christened it "Bronzeville." The residents displayed much civic pride in the community even though they did not necessarily live there by choice. Except for other black enclaves in the city, they were not allowed to live anywhere else in Chicago.

It is ironic that Chicago, which has the reputation of being the most segregated city in the United States, was founded by a black man, Jean Baptiste DuSable. A freedman or fugitive slave from Kentucky, he was the first permanent resident of what is now Chicago. He owned his land on the banks of the Chicago River not by buying it from anyone or getting a grant from the government. His ownership was based on "allodial title," which was conferred by the fact that he lived there, worked the land, and defended it. The trading post he built in 1790 made him a wealthy man. In 1800, he sold his property, which included a house, two barns, a horse-drawn mill, a bakehouse, a poultry house, a dairy, and a smokehouse. His house was only a twenty-two-foot by forty-foot log cabin but it was filled with fine furniture and paintings.

Homes Occupied by Black People, South Chicago. Photo credit: Mary Faith Adams, *Present Housing Conditions in South Chicago, South Deering and Pullman*, Chicago, 1926, 64.

The years that followed DuSable's founding of Chicago and his personal and financial success were years in which the anti-slavery movement in the United States grew strong. Abolitionist societies which were formed all over the country and the anti-slavery movement at large were met with legal challenges and violence. Active societies formed in Illinois in spite of a law condemning them that had been passed by the Illinois General Assembly in 1837.

The purpose of many members of these societies was to keep the institution of slavery out of Illinois. Many of them supported the idea that free-born or freed blacks should be deported to Liberia, a country off the west coast of Africa. Liberia was established on land acquired for freed US slaves by the American Colonization Society. Over the course of its existence, the Society transported 12,000 black people to the colony.

While the anti-slavery movement was strong in Chicago, it did not extend to include freedom and equality for the nearly 1,000 black people making their homes there in 1860. In a small area on the south edge of the Loop, fugitive slaves from the South and free blacks from the East lived among people who were also deemed "undesirable" such as Jewish immigrants from Russia and Poland. The area covered forty-seven acres built up with wooden buildings. A disastrous fire in 1874, three years after the big Chicago fire of 1871, killed twenty people and burned 812 structures. Some of the people who lost their homes and businesses moved farther south from the Loop into the area that became known as the Black Belt, while others moved to the other black enclaves in the city. Likewise, the Jewish people dispersed to other Jewish communities on the Near Westside or north of the Loop.

By 1900, blacks suffered an extraordinary degree of segregation and the residential confinement was nearly complete. Confining black people to a certain area is accomplished not only by putting restrictions on owning property but with physical barriers. Typically, race-conscious communities all over the country used and continue to use railroad tracks, expressways, and rivers to wall off populations of people of color. Lake Michigan served Chicago as the eastern boundary of the ghetto until recently when people of wealth and influence realized that glorious views of the lake are part of the environment of the Black Belt.

The Stroll, a popular spot for black people, was on State Street and extended from 26th Street to 39th Street during the 1910s and 1920s. It was home to dance halls, clubs, restaurants, and movie and vaudeville theaters, and was a center for black businesses such as stores and banks. At night the lights blazed and the streets were crowded with people, black and white, attending various entertainment venues. Black people in their best clothes strolled the streets and took note of each other. The only other place in Chicago where they could be at such ease was in their churches. The Stroll and church were places where they could forget for a while the discrimination and limitations placed on their day-to-day existence.

After the Civil War, states instituted Jim Crow laws which mandated the segregation of public schools, public places, and public transportation, and the separation of restrooms, restaurants, and drinking fountains for whites and blacks. Crossing these lines often resulted in lynchings. These were not just hangings; they included all kinds of violent attacks on and torture of black people young and old.

Hattie's parents were in the vanguard of a great surge of migration from the South to the North and to the West in 1917. This migration drained the South of more than six million people and swelled the populations of northern cities in particular. Some scholars describe this mass movement as one Great Migration that occurred between 1916 and 1970. Other historians divide it into two migrations: one from 1916 to 1930 and another from 1930 to 1970. Between 1916 and 1920, fifty thousand black Southerners moved to Chicago.[31]

The people who made up the first migration were not only fleeing prejudice and violence in the South, they were seeking a better life for themselves and their children. Most hoped to find gainful employment and good schools. Some dreamed that even as adults they would be able to get a good education in night schools in Chicago. The *Chicago Defender*, a black-owned newspaper that circulated widely in the South, published stories about the opportunities in the North.

A confluence of two other events encouraged people to leave the South— a labor surplus and a labor shortage. There was a labor surplus in the South because an infestation of the cotton boll weevil forced a reduction in the acreage devoted to cotton. There was a labor shortage in industrial cities because of the production demands of World War I.

The number of available jobs in war-related industries was increasing as millions of white men were drafted into the military. Adding to the labor shortage was the fact that the number of immigrants from Europe who previously came for such jobs decreased because fears of dangerous immigrants caused Congress to enact legislation limiting the number of immigrants allowed to enter the country. Most of the labor force of

---

31 Christopher Manning, "African Americans," *The Electronic Encyclopedia of Chicago* (Chicago: Chicago Historical Society, 2005), http://www.encyclopedia.chicagohistory.org/pages/27.html.

Chicago had been made up of these immigrants. The earliest to come to Chicago were Germans, Irish, and Scandinavians. After 1880 there were increasing numbers of Poles, Lithuanians, Czechs, Italians, and Eastern European Jews. Jobs in the steel, shipbuilding, automotive, and meat packing industries opened up for black workers.

Many of the European immigrants had at best a tenuous hold on their jobs. Consequently, they feared blacks as competition for jobs in the factories. Their fear was based not only on the increasing number of people competing for jobs but also because employers frequently used blacks as strikebreakers. The fears of white people of whatever ethnicity were accentuated by the rise of racist ideology in Chicago and nationwide that reinforced attitudes that declared blacks to be lazy, unreliable, and slow. The white population grew more and more anxious and agitated as the number of black migrants increased rapidly.

The Second Great Migration (1941-1970) continued to swell the population in the Black Belt. When Hattie was born in 1922, the Black Belt was three miles long by one-quarter of a mile wide. It extended from 22nd Street to 55th Street between Wentworth and Cottage Grove. Her childhood home was in Hyde Park on the very southern border of the Black Belt.

Back Steps of Apartments in Negro Section of Chicago, Illinois. Photo credit: Russell Lee, 1941. https://www.loc.gov/item/2017743593/

In 1922, the total population of Chicago was 2.7 million, with almost 110,000 of the citizens being black. Approximately 85 percent of those 110,000 lived in the Black Belt. Another smaller colony existed on the West Side, and smaller black enclaves were scattered over parts of Chicago farther south. However, the challenges of the Black Belt related to housing, education, and work opportunities also applied to these other areas.

By 1930, the area from 22nd Street to 63rd Street between Wentworth and Cottage Grove was solidly black. During the Great Depression, migration decreased dramatically. From the 1930s to the 1940s, there were only slight territorial additions, but that changed when the US entered the Second World War in December 1941. The great need to replace men in industry who were serving in the military and the need for accelerated production of war material drew people from the South to Chicago and other industrial cities. Between 1940 and 1960, Chicago's black population grew from 278,000 to 813,000.[32]

The segregation of black people was carried out with the support of all levels of government. Public policy in the form of "restrictive covenants" determined where the races could buy homes. Restrictive covenants were clauses added to property titles by which an individual buyer entered into a community-wide compact not to sell or lease his or her property to certain classes of people. These classes of people were predominantly blacks but also frequently included Jewish people and Asians. A property owner who held such a title was prohibited from selling the property to these specific people. In addition, lenders, including federal agencies, would not give mortgages to blacks who wanted to buy property in a "covenanted" area. Further exacerbating the problem, insurers would not provide insurance to blacks who wanted to buy in a "covenanted" neighborhood. These practices maintained the exclusivity of traditionally white neighborhoods.[33] Between 1927 and 1929, almost four and a half miles of the Black Belt were covered by restrictive covenants. By 1948, this area had grown to more than eleven square miles. That year restrictive covenants were declared constitutionally unenforceable by the Supreme Court, but the practice of keeping blacks out of white neighborhoods continued.

In 1927, the *Hyde Park Herald* newspaper described the restrictive covenants in glowing terms: "a marvelous delicately woven chain of armor" from "the northern Gates of Hyde Park at 35th and Drexel Boulevard to the South Side…of Chicago."[34] Even Al Capone's mother signed up to guarantee the "respectability" of the family home.[35]

During the 1940s, an abundance of jobs existed in the stockyards, railroads, and factories, but everything started to change after the war ended. Several factors contributed to the decrease in jobs. One was the rapid growth of the federal highway system and the development of refriger-

---

32 Manning, "African Americans."
33 Pattillo, *Black on the Block*, 319n48.
34 Quoted in Arnold R. Hirsch, "Restrictive Covenants," *Encyclopedia of Chicago Online, 2005*, http://www.encyclopedia.chicagohistory.org/pages/1067.html.
35 Hirsch, "Restrictive Covenants."

ated trucks, which made it possible for these industries to move out of the expensive urban areas which had in the past provided them access to railroad shipping. With the new ease of shipping meat, meat packers built mechanized plants in less expensive rural areas. This allowed them to do business directly with the farmers who provided the livestock, thus eliminating the need for the stockyards which had earned Chicago the title "Hog Butcher of the World." Other exacerbating factors were an increase in land value, rising property taxes, and antipollution laws within the city of Chicago.

When we met Hattie in the 1980s, her neighborhood was hemmed in by the Stevenson Expressway on the north, the Dan Ryan Expressway and railroad tracks on the west, Hyde Park and the University of Chicago on the south, and Lake Michigan and its beaches to the east. A few of her neighbors lived in stand-alone homes which they either owned or rented, but the greatest number of her neighbors lived in public housing. At one point Bronzeville included several of the poorest census tracts in the nation.

The ghetto of Bronzeville was shaped by the determination, strength, and optimism of its black citizens in the face of cruelty, discrimination, and segregation. Being denied housing elsewhere in the city and being limited in places to shop, black people responded by building businesses and institutions of their own within the rigid boundaries imposed on them. During the decades of the 1910s and 1920s, the ghetto, also labeled the Black Belt, was a vibrant area where property owners and community leaders maintained black-owned businesses and churches, and hotels and theaters proliferated. Citizens of the area enjoyed picnics, parades, and concerts.

Among the black citizens there was a wide range of income levels from the wealthy to those who lived in extreme poverty. However, the class structure was based more on how long one had lived in Chicago. Residents who lived there before the Great Migration largely looked with disdain on the newly arrived folks from the South who tended to be rural in their dress and behavior. In the midst of all this, there was a richness to black family life that stemmed from family groupings and church connections.

In spite of the richness of its culture, Bronzeville's fortunes began to decline in the 1960s and 1970s. The 1948 Supreme Court ruling that restrictive covenants were unconstitutional was a good thing in the sense that real estate agents could not require people to sign a covenant. However, a downside was that it caused a decline in population because black people who could afford to move left the neighborhood and moved to the suburbs, although the areas where they were accepted were still limited. The people who had to stay were the folks in the decades-old private and public housing who had little money to spend even on groceries and health care. Not only were people moving out of Bronzeville, at the same time local businesses were losing many of their customers to well-capitalized downtown and suburban competitors that were newly opening their doors to black customers. With their paying customers decreasing, businesses such as grocery stores, drugstores, clothing stores, and theaters closed or moved out.

Several other factors contributed to the decline of Bronzeville. One was the placement of large numbers of publicly subsidized housing units which brought many additional low-income residents to the community. Another was the sealing off of this area by limiting people's access to communities of richer opportunities through the construction of the Dan Ryan Expressway. Still another factor was the negative impact on Chicago's economy due to the decline of the stockyards and the steel mills.

The building of the Dan Ryan Expressway made traveling to and through Chicago faster and easier, but it acted as a wall that, along with Lake Michigan, served as a boundary enclosing the poverty-stricken residents of Bronzeville. The expressway became a barrier between the black neighborhood where opportunities for people were disappearing and the white neighborhoods where opportunities were blossoming.

For decades the Black Belt has been a target of developers because of its unobstructed views of Lake Michigan and proximity to the shopping and entertainment options available in the Loop. The goal of real estate developers, city planners, and politicians was to replace that area of "blight" with what they term "mixed-income" communities. The pretext was to "raise up" black slum dwellers by having them live among white (or black) people who worked for a living and thus would set a good example for them. In theory, the more affluent would model how to hold down a job, how to take care of one's children, and how to maintain one's property.

Hattie spoke about this redevelopment with Olin Eugene Myers, a student at the University of Chicago who interviewed her for a class assignment in 1986. He asked her if it was the city that was doing this. She first laid blame on the University of Chicago, Michael Reese Hospital, and the Illinois Institute of Technology. All three institutions needed more and more land, on which to house their expanding service. They also wanted to be surrounded by neighborhoods where white people would not be afraid to come. About the city, she said:

> I am familiar with the city because I was born on this very street. I've seen the tactics—how redevelopment plans come through. It's not just against blacks. I've seen whole Polish and Lithuanian neighborhoods moved out, en masse here to make room for an expressway, you know, the Stevenson, the Eisenhower. And so I don't necessarily label it as black, but I know the whole mechanism of what happens when a neighborhood is going to be redeveloped and how it's done and how the people are duped and put out. So the Projects are being cleared now.[36]

Hattie predicted in the 1980s that in ten years all the people from the public housing would be gone. Her prediction was accurate. The public housing was demolished, leaving one thousand people homeless. The rundown area that was Hattie's neighborhood is now a place of parks and avenues connecting new two-story homes and thriving franchise businesses. Common sense says this is progress, a good thing, but a burning question still remains: where have all the people gone? Where do their children and their children's children live now?

Today, looking at real estate webpages and at Chicago's Plan for Transformation, it is obvious that most of "her people" are gone. Their homes—public and private—have been replaced by what is touted as "mixed income" neighborhoods.

Two of the high-rise public housing buildings across the street from Hattie's home have been renovated and renamed. When they housed

---

36 Myers, interview, 5.

poor black people, they were called the Lake Park Properties. They are now Lake Parc Place and contain three hundred units of both rental and privately-owned apartments and condominiums. Seven hundred poor black families were evicted from these buildings.

Hattie's House in 2015.
Used by permission: Beverly Jane Phillips.

Hattie's house was valued at about $20,000 when she lived there. Realtors' estimates in 2019 are set at $450,000. One realtor's page described it as a huge house, 2,564 square feet, built in 1883, that you could turn into your "mini-mansion." The mansions of the rich and famous of Chicago are gone from the area as are most of the public housing that replaced them. Now the redeveloped buildings can again be called mansions.

Chapter 5
SHALOM COMMUNITY

Hattie's story would be incomplete if it didn't include the Rev. Dr. Claude Marie Barbour and Shalom Community, a cross-cultural ministry. Claude Marie and Hattie were of the same mind about how best to help people trapped in poverty in the ghetto that was Kenwood/Oakland. Many churches and charitable organizations came into Oakland with their own ideas about what would benefit the neighborhood. Hattie said, "I felt someone should say, 'What are your needs? We will help you.'" This feeling that the recipients should be able to tell people what they themselves felt they needed help with led to her idea of mission-in-reverse. This was a concept that encouraged people from outside the ghetto to come to visit, to see the needs for themselves, and to listen to the people who lived in such poverty-stricken conditions.

"On Widow's Pension, She Helps Poor." (undated clipping), *Sun-Times*. Photo credit: Bob Black. Used by permission: *Chicago Sun-Times*.

Hattie said in an interview:

> I began the work of Shalom in this house through faith. I think the faith stemmed from the miraculous recovery from my first brain operation in 1966. I had an idea of a cross-cultural ministry. I did not know how to implement this ministry, but I knew that it was something that should happen. I felt that God would open doors that I am unable to see, but I didn't know how. So I had no one to give my ideas to, but I like to write so I just put them in a book, a Bible, when I finished writing my idea of a cross-cultural ministry.

> A ministry which would entail black teachers and people who would come, would be, as I call it, the reachers. For once, the mission-in-reverse concept would work just the opposite, that people would come into a low-income black community; I call this Third World USA because our statistics border on third world countries.[37]

Almost a decade later, Hattie discovered to her amazement that there was such a program already in existence.

> With that, I did not know how you could implement a cross-cultural program, but as I am a widow and I raised six children in this house, I decided rather than suffer empty nest syndrome, to be about my Father's business. So I just prayed and put it in the Bible and then [1979] one of the nuns (I'm Catholic) who had a class at the Catholic Theological Union said she wanted to introduce me to an instructor there who thought a lot like I did, because she knew some of my thoughts and ideas…she introduced me to Dr. Claude Marie Barbour. It turned out that she is an ordained Presbyterian minister, a French Huguenot, and she was teaching with tenure in a Catholic institution! I said, now how on earth can we think alike or have anything in common if this be the case, because I am a black woman, born and raised on Lake Park, lived on one street all my life. How can I think as an instructor, an educator, a minister, not even an American, as you might say, and all of this in a Catholic institution? But I went to meet Dr. Claude Marie Barbour, and a thought came to me just as I went out of the door, go back, get your paper out of your Bible, and take it with you and show it to her as you meet her. Claude Marie read the paper and she had implemented a program very similar in Gary, Indiana working with Hispanics and blacks…So with that, we both knew that the Lord had joined us two unlikely women in a work. We then established a satellite [in Hattie's home], or part of the Shalom program which has a philosophy of people who come to serve and actually learn from the people. This was the exact philosophies and ideas that I had

---

37 Edwards, interview, 1.

on paper, so it was like coming together, and we both established the Shalom community in the black community.³⁸

When Hattie Williams and Claude Marie Barbour were introduced to each other it was truly a meeting of soul sisters! They were, in Hattie's words, "two unlikely women in a work." Claude Marie was born in Belgium in 1935. Hattie was born in Chicago in 1922. One was white. One was black. One had theological degrees. One had a social work degree. One had lived in South Africa. One had lived her whole life on South Lake Park Avenue in Chicago. The one similarity that brought them together was the calling of their beloved God to serve others.

As a young girl in France, Claude Marie felt called to mission work. After she completed her studies in nursing she undertook her first mission assignment in the early 1960s in Lesotho, in southern Africa, and for a time in Soweto, South Africa. In South Africa, she ministered to Bantu people and was imprisoned for spending the night in a township taking care of orphaned children—breaking the apartheid law that forbade a white person from being in a black neighborhood overnight. When she was rescued by Amnesty International she came to the United States and studied at New York Theological Seminary, earning a Master's degree in Systematic Theology. She later completed her doctorate in Systematic Theology at Garrett-Evangelical Theological Seminary in Evanston, Illinois. During that time she worked at First Presbyterian Church in Gary, Indiana. She was ordained to the office of Minister of Word and Sacrament in the Presbyterian Church (USA) in 1974.³⁹

It was her work in the racially diverse and divided Gary that called her to the attention of the mission faculty at Catholic Theological Union, McCormick Seminary, and Lutheran School of Theology, a consortium of theological schools in Chicago. All three institutions were in need of someone to help train their students for mission and cross-cultural ministry. She was appointed Professor of World Mission at the Catholic Theological Union in 1976. She is now Professor of World Mission, Emerita. She taught and worked in the area of reconciliation, healing, and ministry among refugees and survivors of human rights abuses. Her teaching and mentoring of missionary and ministry students and oth-

---

38 Edwards, interview, 1.
39 "Rev. Dr. Claude Marie Barbour," Faculty, Catholic Theological Union, https://ctu.edu/faculty/claude-barbour/.

ers were modeled after her own ministry with groups and individuals. Claude Marie's theological and missionary commitment, interests, and research still focus on ecumenism, interfaith dialogue, intercultural relations, and the intersection of gospel and culture.

She has ministered among the Lakota and Oglala Sioux on the Rosebud and Pine Ridge reservations in South Dakota. Practicing mission-in-reverse for more than three decades, she coordinated course and field placements in Native American and refugee communities in Chicago and South Dakota.

In 1973 she founded Shalom Ministries, an ecumenical covenant community giving special emphasis to the training and preparation of their own members and others for mission and ministry in a global context. Shalom's mission statement reads:

> Seeking to live as followers of Christ,
>
> We, the workers of Shalom
>
> will strive to be signs of unity, reconciliation and healing
>
> in a broken world, and to work for justice and peace.
>
> When there is division, we seek to be bridges,
>
> to carry the burdens of others,
>
> sharing concretely in their sufferings,
>
> to take risks, never standing still, to be signs of joy and love,
>
> to be present and open, ready to receive as well as to give,
>
> freeing us all to become who we are meant to be.[40]

Currently, there are many Shalom communities in all parts of the world. Members of Shalom are committed to practicing a simple lifestyle among people with whom they work, particularly the poor, oppressed, and marginalized.

---

40 Bevans, Doidge, Schreiter, *The Healing Circle*, 201.

When Claude Marie began to think of mission-in-reverse as a way of doing ministry she was in Lesotho, living among and ministering to Bantu people. It was a long way from her girlhood in France where she was raised by Huguenot parents who were committed to their faith. They were also committed to the ethical values of the people of Le Chambon, a Protestant village in the South of France where some five thousand Jews fleeing the Nazis were given refuge.

When Hattie's ministry and home became a Shalom Community it greatly expanded the work she was doing. Clergy and laity from suburban churches came to Hattie's home and neighborhood to listen and learn, to become the "reachers," as Hattie put it, with the neighborhood people serving as their "teachers." Nuns came to live in a neighboring apartment, and priests and Catholic and Protestant seminary students came to live in Hattie's home. They were there to listen to the people in order to discover from them their needs and what could be done to meet those needs. It was indeed mission-in-reverse.

Hattie admitted that it was not an easy thing for white people to do:

> In the cross-cultural ministry in this house people of other ethnic backgrounds, the majority white come here they go through culture shock. They're in a totally black environment, strange, different race, different culture, different everything. And so they go through this culture shock, and sometimes it's very brief, sometimes it's—I've seen people go through it for two or three months. They end up staying here five years, but it's something that you can't change in that person. You can pray for them, you can watch them, you can expose them, you can show them, take them around. You let them see, you let them come to their own judgment.[41]

What they were doing seems innocent enough but Hattie was taking big risks. Part of her ministry was to have white nuns, priests, and seminary students live in the neighborhood, so naturally Hattie found places for them to live. She housed three men in her own home. It was risky because they were white people in a black neighborhood where drugs, gangs, and crime were rampant. Another risk she took was that of rob-

---
41 Myers, interview, 55.

bery because the constant arrival and distribution of used household items, clothing, and food made her home a target for thieves. Hattie was not naïve about these risks, but she was determined to speak her Lord's message in word and in deed.

Hattie led the members of the Shalom Community to see and learn through a multitude of activities. Under her direction, they provided direct services to the people through a clothing closet and a food pantry which were located in the basement of her home. Church groups from the white suburbs frequently brought food and clothing to help supply the closet and pantry. Self-help efforts such as sewing and budgeting classes and vegetable gardening in vacant lots were conducted. A General Educational Development (GED) program was organized to help adults earn their high school diplomas. Not only did members of the Shalom community encourage people to attend welfare hearings to voice their concerns, but they also accompanied them to the hearings. Since aldermen are the most influential political figures in the neighborhoods, Hattie and her protégés would bring in aldermen and other city legislators to listen to neighborhood grievances. Hattie hosted weekly meetings at which residents came together to share concerns, plan joint actions, and simply pray together. Anywhere from a dozen to thirty people of all ages would gather every Saturday for these sharing sessions.

Marlene Perrotte, RSM, and Elise Saggau, OSF, two theology students in seminaries on the south side of Chicago in Hattie's neighborhood, worked with Hattie in the Shalom Community. One of their projects was to organize summer activities for the children who lived in the high-rise public housing buildings across the street from Hattie's home. Sister Elise described playgrounds that the Chicago Housing Authority built near the high-rises as a serious hazard. Although they had swings, slides, teeter-totters, and climbing bars, the surface beneath this equipment was solid concrete covered in broken glass. Marlene and Elise observed children playing on the open walkways that ran level with each floor of the fifteen-story high-rises, in the parking lot, and in the street, because as dangerous as those places were, they were safer than the playgrounds.

One bright spot in a hot summer was when someone would turn on one of the fire hydrants and let the children play in the cool water. Without a plan of their own, the two women asked people gathered at Hattie's if they would be willing to work with the children during the summer.

From February until May they listened to the residents and found out from the mothers that they wanted constructive and safe activities and a guided program. There were too many children to serve, so acceptance into the program was based on a parent or guardian who would be willing and able to help. Sixty children were registered and the program began. In addition to parents helping, eight qualified teenagers from the neighborhood received Comprehensive Employment and Training Act (CETA) compensation for working in the program. Over the summer, with no printed resources, the nuns, parents, teenagers, and volunteers from nearby seminaries and churches provided summer activities for sixty children between the ages of three to eighteen.

At the end of the month when Marlene and Elise had to leave, the parents successfully continued the program for another three weeks. In addition, the CETA students formed a group called Shalom Juniors and served, under Hattie's direction, on other neighborhood projects. One of the seminarians who lived in Hattie's home was Roger Schroeder, who is now a Professor of Mission and Culture in the Department of Intercultural Studies and Ministry at the Catholic Theological Union where he was a student from 1974-1976. In a recent phone interview, he described the work of Hattie as being very "holistic."

When Schroeder came to work with her, Hattie assigned him to work with the young men in the community. Schroeder said he would never have done this on his own—a white man working with young black men, some of whom were newly released from jail. During the summer, he met with the young men in the basement of one of the public housing high-rises. Together with Hattie, they organized a football team. True to her experience of an answered prayer, Hattie prayed for football uniforms and equipment, and a suburban church provided them.

Schroeder also remembers that Hattie had a beautiful singing voice and played the piano very well. Many evenings were spent with Hattie and her residents singing to Hattie's playing and in prayer.[42]

The nuns and priests who became part of Hattie's mission-in-reverse came not with ideas about what was needed by the people but with skills and talents that were useful when people said they needed them. One

---

42 Roger Schroeder, phone interview with author, June 8, 2016.

of the students from Catholic Theological Seminary taught drywall and plastering to a group of men:

> Sometimes, even if they're not working, they're observing, and they're learning and sometimes in finding out the root causes of what you would say, "well, why are these guys standing around shooting craps, they're drinking wine, and that they're lazy, and they're not looking for work?" Then, if you live here and you can hang around the housing units and listen to these guys talk a while, and then you would see underneath that, how much effort they have put in trying to fill out a job application when they couldn't read, or how many efforts they had made to find employment. It explodes some of the myths you might have regarding them.[43]

Hattie's ministry even extended to gardening. In 1981, an Illinois farmer gave Hattie a truckload of rich black soil. With the advice of an extension agent from the University of Illinois Extension Service in Cook County,[44] Hattie and her neighbors planted a vegetable garden on an abandoned lot. The vegetables grew and produced food to be shared among the gardeners. One extremely unusual result was, in Hattie's words, "carrots as round as radishes." There was concrete under the imported rich soil!

The seminarians, nuns, and priests reaped rich rewards from their contact with the people of Oakland. Julie Bruska, one of the members of Shalom, expressed her learning in this way:

> I lived there for 15 months. Hattie and her neighbors were so incredibly gracious in taking in someone like me, who didn't know the ropes at all. People were terribly patient in letting me see the problems through their eyes. I realized that if the world is going to be transformed, all of us have to change. It's not a matter of "changing those people." We have to learn to hear each other.[45]

---

44 The Extension Service was founded in Land Grant Universities around the country based on the belief that knowledge can change lives. The agents offered practical education to solve problems and develop skills in homemaking, agriculture, and animal husbandry.
45 Helen Post, "Claude Marie Barbour: God Calls Us to Live in Solidarity with People who Represent the Suffering Christ," *Testimony* 2 (Summer 88): unpaged.

Hattie described Shalom to me and others with these words: "While leaning on the Lord, we are bringing some residents and workers to a new awareness. We've got to listen, learn, and help. That's grass-roots, getting-back-to-basics for us and for Shalom, which reached out to become part of our neighborhood."

Hattie likened the growth of Shalom ministries to the summer spread of dandelions in Kenwood. "Shalom is coming up between the cracks in the concrete. Have you ever seen those little seeds from the dandelion? They blow all over, and they gotta land somewhere!"

Chapter 6
PUBLIC HOUSING

When Hattie and Bernard bought their house in Bronzeville at 4064 South Lake Park Avenue in the middle of the 1940s, the housing around them ranged from grand mansions on Drexel Boulevard to decaying slum buildings on South Indiana Street. Their house would have been somewhere in the middle of these two extremes. It was a two-story Victorian-style house flanked by houses of similar design and vintage. Built in 1883, it had fifteen rooms, an attic, and a basement. Across the street was the Oakenwald Elementary school where Hattie's children were students. The lots were narrow and deep. Front lawns were lined with ornamental wrought iron fences. The politics of their city and their country were about to change their neighborhood beyond recognition.

The history of Chicago's struggle to provide housing for its black citizens is long, complicated, and continuing. It is a patchwork of good intentions and greed, of high ideals and political reality, of liberalism and conservatism, of integration and segregation. For decades this patchwork housing program was stitched together and came apart as federal, state, and local officials made policy and spent money on urban renewal, also known as slum clearance or, in the words of the writer James Baldwin, "Negro removal."

During the 1800s big cities all over the country housed poverty-stricken people of many races and ethnicities in substandard conditions. The physical aspects of the tenements differed from city to city. In New York City the typical housing in the slums, as they were called, was six- or seven-story walkups which covered whole city blocks. Typical slum housing for the poor in Chicago was two- to four-story wooden buildings crowded onto small lots.

In these wooden buildings, rooms were dark and airless because houses were built so close to each other that rooms had no windows to let in light and air. On many lots a house was built on the front of the lot and another house on the back of the same lot. Some were built lower than the level of the streets and sidewalks. As a result, rainwater, snowmelt, and sewage washed into these homes. Outdoor privies served as toilet facilities. No space was left for playgrounds or parks, so children played on the sidewalks, in the streets, or in the sewers. The poor people who lived in rented housing in the slums didn't dare complain. If they did there would most likely be one of two results: their rent would be increased or they would be evicted.

After the Great Chicago Fire of 1871, the building of wooden structures in the city was prohibited. Thus, the wooden buildings that housed the poor and various immigrant communities were built on what was then the outskirts of the city. Thousands of European immigrants lived in ethnic slums in Chicago but conditions were worse for blacks because racial boundaries were energetically defended by whites.

As studies in public health developed after the Civil War, public health professionals collected data on the worst housing districts in the United States. These studies demonstrated that infant mortality and disease were directly connected to windowless rooms, improper ventilation, and little or very poor plumbing. Cities were convinced by the reformers to hire public health inspectors for the tenements and to force improvements, but the scope of the problem was far too massive for cities to handle.

By the end of the nineteenth century, progressives were asserting that poor housing did not only cause disease but also fostered juvenile delinquency and illegal behavior that resulted in greater crime and increased societal breakdown. Two reformers who had national impact were Jane Addams (1860-1935) in Chicago and Jacob Riis (1849-1914) in New York City. Hattie always expressed great admiration for Jane Addams, taking her as a model for caring for and advocating for marginalized people. Addams, known as the "mother" of social work founded Hull House in Chicago as a place where European immigrants to Chicago could learn how to function in the city. She launched a crusade for better housing through her writing and speaking. Jacob Riis focused the spotlight on the terrible living conditions of the slums using the new flash photography technology invented in 1888. He took pictures in dark corners of alleyways and tenements, exposing the desperate conditions of the people who lived in the squalor of the slums.

Reformers wanted government to intervene because they believed the government could provide public housing for people who were too poor to buy or rent in the private housing market. They recognized that this was a thorny idea that quite possibly could overstep the bounds of the rights of property owners. The reformers had no intention of displacing legitimate private landlords and good quality housing for all people who could afford it. To overcome this threat to private landlords the idea of "market failure" became the justification for government intervention. The idea was that the market should provide decent, livable housing for all people. Market failure happened when people couldn't afford to pay a market rate rent or a market rate purchase price. Thus, the fact that so many people lived in slum housing was a glaring market failure. Poor people couldn't afford anything better than the housing found in the slums. Black people were doubly hindered by their poverty and their color.

Not only did the market failure concept open the possibility of government intervention, it also determined who could be served by public housing and affected design and construction costs. In order that the private market would not be threatened, public housing had to be low cost and thus low quality. It had to be as cheap as authorities could make it.

Federal action in housing was a looming fear in Chicago. Few seemed to mind when in 1934 the federal government interfered in the housing market by creating the Federal Housing Administration (FHA), whose purpose was to guarantee private housing loans and prop up the homebuilding industry. Three years later Congress passed the Housing Act of 1937, which was meant to serve the same purpose for public housing as the FHA did for private housing. Instead of loans for homes for those who could afford them, it provided for subsidies to be paid from the United States government to local housing agencies in order to provide better housing for low-income citizens.

This act established three dominant principles that defined public housing for decades. The first principle of the Housing Act of 1937 was that federal and local authorities would work together to build the housing. It gave the selection of sites for public housing to local authorities. Site selection was a hornets' nest of conflict. On the one hand, progressive reformers wanted the building of public housing to be an anti-poverty program that would rebuild slums for the benefit of the people who lived in them. On the other hand, modern city planners of the time wanted a nonprofit building program on vacant land for the working class. The coalition of these two groups proposed both plans to Congress but the reformers in Chicago wanted to clear the unsanitary living conditions of the slums altogether. So, large tracts of land were cleared of the slum housing and high-rise public buildings replaced them in a process called "urban renewal."

The "Neighborhood Composition Rule," a federal rule passed in 1935, had banned projects from altering the existing racial composition of their neighborhoods. The rule was that the race of the occupants of a completed project had to conform to the race of the surrounding neighborhood. This policy kept whites from reclaiming areas that had become black and avoided clashes with segregationists. It reassured white people that the federal government would not demand integration or "color blind" tenant selection in renting apartments in projects. This rule stayed in effect until 1949, which was long enough to entrench the segregation that has been typical of public housing.

The second principle of the Housing Act of 1937 was that the federal government would subsidize the building of the housing. Subsidies amounting to 90 percent of the cost, in the form of construction loans, were given to local housing and noncommercial groups to cover the costs of building. These loans came from the sale of US Treasury Bonds at favorable rates.

Along with the loans, the federal government would make an "annual contribution" to local housing authorities. These were yearly cash payments made to the local housing authorities in order to reduce rents to affordable levels. The annual contribution was meant to cover the cost of the loans (subsidies) made to the builders and the interest they accrued. This provision amounted to the federal government paying for the entire cost of public housing built by local housing authorities. The federal government made the loans and then gave the housing authorities the money to pay off the loans. Such a plan opened the way for local greed, graft, and mismanagement. In essence and in fact, it meant that Chicago got its public housing free.

The third principle of the Housing Act of 1937 was that rents would be set with two social goals in mind. One was to raise the standard of living for low-income families by getting them out of unhealthy, hazardous housing with the expectation that living in better homes would improve their health and well-being. The second goal was to increase people's self-esteem as individuals and thus improve their communities.

The Chicago Housing Authority was established by Mayor Edward Kelly as a result of the Housing Act of 1937. Mayor Kelly sympathized with the plight of black citizens and their needs, so he appointed a board with a good representation of nonpartisan experts which made it progressive. Over the years the Chicago Housing Authority backed housing reform and after a few years championed the civil rights of African Americans. As would be expected in Chicago, a city marked by racism and government corruption, there were also periods when self-interested politics drove the actions of the housing authority.

After Japan attacked Pearl Harbor on December 7, 1941, the war industry in the United States burgeoned, drawing thousands of migrants to Chicago and other northern industrial cities. As a result, the United States Housing Authority projects were pressed into service as housing for war workers. The debate over how to determine rents became more and more problematic. The choice was between fixed rates, a fixed amount per month, or rates based on a percentage of the renter's income.

The fixed rate plan was good for people whose income was in a higher range and held the possibility of increasing because even if their income increased their rent stayed the same. However, it left very poor families paying more than 20 percent of their income for rent, which left very little for other necessities. When the rent was a percentage of income, poor people paid lower rent while people of high income paid more.

The US Housing Authority urged local housing authorities to choose the income-based rents for two reasons. One was that it pushed people whose income was increasing out of public housing into the private market, thus opening apartments for poorer families. The other reason was that it lessened the rent burden of the poorer residents. However, setting low rents turned out to be a mixed blessing. Renters with low income and thus lower rents turned out to be mostly black people. A downside was that lower rents made it more difficult for the Chicago Housing Authority to maintain the buildings.

The design of public housing buildings was also an issue of great consequence. The two top criteria of the federal housing program were that it had to be cheap and plain. One administrator of the US Housing Authority decreed that there would be no "frills" in any public housing buildings. Engineers in Washington, DC, built a laboratory that consisted of a full-size apartment with movable walls. These walls were moved in inch by inch to determine the minimum space required to accommodate the furnishings a family needed to live. The US Housing Authority even recommended as another cost-cutting measure that closet doors be omitted and curtain rods be supplied. That would save forty dollars per unit.

The cost obsession in Washington, DC, caused the Chicago Housing Authority to build high-rise buildings of fifteen to twenty stories. They were cheaper to build than one or two-story buildings because more units could be built on less land than row houses would require. They were also cheaper to build because they had common walls and roofs, plumbing, and heating. The construction of long parallel rows of buildings reduced the cost for interior streets and walkways, but this design made the areas extremely hard to police.

These principles and designs created a readily identifiable government housing look. At first, this look labeled the people who lived there as poor and later labeled them as black. The equating of public housing as black housing happened between 1945 and 1966 when the Chicago Housing Authority built 23,400 apartments for low-income families, which were nearly all in black neighborhoods.

The Robert Taylor Homes were a prime example of this cost-controlling tactic. Robert Taylor, the justice-minded chairman of the Chicago Housing Authority in 1942, would have opposed these high-rises, but he died in 1957. Built in 1962, these homes consisted of twenty-eight buildings of sixteen stories each which stretched for two miles along the Dan Ryan Expressway. There was a total of 4,415 units, mostly arranged in U-shaped clusters of three. Six of the poorest US census areas with populations above 2,500 were found there. It was planned for 11,000 inhabitants, but at its peak the Robert Taylor Homes housed up to 27,000 people, 20,000 of them children.

Along with unemployment and low income, the very construction of the buildings fostered gangs and a high crime rate that plagued the families who lived there as well as causing problems for police and firefighters. Access to the buildings was difficult because of the lack of interior streets. Crime inside the buildings was hard to address because of the number of people living there and the lack of reliable elevator service.

During the decade of the 1960s, various attempts were made by federal and city governments to make public housing more equitable and to give people more freedom in choosing where they would live. In 1961, the Housing Act of 1937 was amended to create a program whereby low-income people could receive a subsidy to enable them to rent a home in the private market. Under Section 23, as it was called, qualified low-income tenants paid a portion of the rent that an owner might get in the open market and the housing authority paid the balance.

Chicago's City Council, after a heated debate, passed its own Fair Housing Act in 1963, ostensibly for the protection of blacks. It prohibited discrimination "against any person because of his race, color, religion, national origin or ancestry" in the quest for housing. Subsequent versions extended protection on the grounds of sex, age, marital and parental status, sexual orientation, disability, source of income, and military discharge status.

Civil rights legislation passed in the 1960s was vital in the struggle for equality for black people. The Civil Rights Act of 1964 outlawed segregation in public places and employment discrimination based on race, color, religion, sex, or national origin. The Voting Rights Act of 1965 enforced the Fifth Amendment of the Constitution, which allowed black men to vote by making illegal any means used to disqualify black voters, such as literacy and language barriers. Another civil rights act, intended as a follow up to the 1964 bill, was passed in 1968. It was popularly called the Fair Housing Act, Title VIII because it prohibited discrimination in the sale, rental, and financing of housing based on race, religion, national origin, or sex. The bill was heatedly discussed in the Senate but was passed quickly in the House of Representatives in the days after the assassination of civil rights leader Martin Luther King Jr. The act stands as the final great legislative achievement of the civil rights era.

The passage of these laws did not prevent real estate agents from finding ways to circumvent them by manipulating blacks and whites who were buying or selling houses. One such practice, called blockbusting, was used to pressure white homeowners to sell their homes at a loss by suggesting that the neighborhood was about to be integrated. Then, the real estate agent would sell the same house at a great profit to a black family who was eager to get out of the ghetto. Another practice was to delay appointments with black individuals in hopes that a white person would buy or rent the property first. Title VIII of the Federal Fair Housing Act outlawed all of these practices.

However, the fair housing laws did not address the tension between people's freedom to choose where they wanted to live and residential racial integration. In 1966 Martin Luther King Jr. spent time in Chicago speaking and demonstrating against segregated housing in Chicago. He and his colleagues met face to face with Mayor Richard M. Daley, but these conversations did not produce many real results. However, King's assassination spurred President Lyndon B. Johnson and Congress to pass the 1968 Fair Housing Act. The return of Vietnam veterans who were in need of housing greatly facilitated the passage of the bill. Since deaths in Vietnam fell heavily on young, poor men, black and Hispanic, the need for housing in segregated areas increased.

Title VIII (commonly known as Section 8) had two parts. The first was a major housing-allowance type program, which provided households with the difference between what they could afford and the Fair Market Rent for an apartment in their area. Tenants would pay 25 percent, which was soon increased to 30 percent, of their income on rent. The second part of Section 8 provided operating subsidies which were supposed to help private builders improve the design of their housing.

The operating subsidies were intended to maintain the public housing buildings, but they were poorly used and mismanaged. Keeping the elevators working was a major problem in the management of the highrise public housing. Hattie often railed about not only the inconvenience of the broken elevators but also about the dangers they posed. In the building across the street from Hattie's home, there were only two sets of elevators to serve the more than one thousand people who lived there in the sixteen stories. With limited places to play, the elevators were prime "toys" for the children of the buildings. They were also the target of vandals.

In 1980 the Chicago Housing Authority maintenance chief admitted that the elevators in all of the high-rise public housing buildings did not work 30 percent of the time. This was a major cost to the CHA not only because the elevators were badly abused by tenants but also because the CHA contracted out the work of repairing them and then did not consistently oversee the workers who were doing the repair and maintenance. Accusations were made that the mechanics failed to perform repairs or that they sabotaged the elevators to make sure they would have return calls. The mechanics defended their actions by saying that their work environment was dangerous and their fudging on hours and repairs amounted to "battle pay."

Hattie said this about the Lake Front Properties public housing across the street from her home. "There's ten apartments on the 16th floor that have not been rented for eight years. For some reason that floor has been left, and it is said it was because they couldn't rig up the elevator to go up there, but thugs know how to rig elevators to go anywhere."[46]

The CHA operated on a triage system as far as repairs to the buildings were concerned. For instance, in 1975 and 1976, it decided that when windows on the lower floors were broken, windows from the vacant upper stories would be removed and used as replacements. Some upper floors had lower occupancy, so plywood was used to cover the open spaces where windows had been removed. Over time the plywood cracked and offered little protection from cold, wind, and snow, making those units costlier to repair if and when they were rented.

Keeping the heating systems working was another major problem for the CHA. Hattie and others saw this as a ploy to get people to move out of their apartments so that the buildings could eventually be razed and replaced with higher income housing. Hattie said that this happened frequently:

> They had no heat at all, the furnace is broke down. And when the furnace is broke down, wouldn't you think that

---

46 Edwards, interview, 15.

any building, if it was the Hancock building, they would have union men repairing that furnace around the clock. With as many children as we have in the building across the street, there was no such effort. The people were without heat in the winter, but they had gas stoves in their apartments. So they burned the gas. It was on TV, every channel ran it, carbon monoxide poisoning and people brought out on stretchers. Thank God there wasn't any deaths.

Well, what would you do if you were freezing cold, below zero? You'd burn the gas too, you would take a chance with that. There was nothing too much that could be done, but after that the Chicago Housing Authority brought everybody a kerosene heater and gave it to them. That would heat one room. Then because the news media was in on it, they came out and did something to the boiler and that lasted two weeks. People had heat for Christmas and after that, "Oh, the boiler broke down."

Wouldn't you think it was a ploy to get people flushed out of the buildings? I felt that way. So what you have now is a remnant of people over here who will take a $50 room and move somewhere. Sometimes they'll take the $50 and get an apartment and divide it up and somebody would live in one part, and somebody would be in the other part, and relatives were bunking together.

What is the next move after this situation as I've seen it, and this does not necessarily mean that blacks were always the ones removed. Here in Chicago, in order to make way for expressways, I have found whole ethnic groups moved out that were not black. Their properties condemned and given a pittance for their houses, and then you have your Stevenson, your Eisenhower, all your expressways.

This is the mechanism of the city, the government. The next step would be, it would not be hard to come into houses such as this and condemn it. Just condemn the house. Find something wrong with it, even if it's a non-existent wrong. They would find some way to say, "Oh, this is unfit for human habitation, we condemn it. Now, we've assessed your property, and it ain't worth nothing. Here, just $5,000 for nuisance value. Now get out of here." And then they redevelop this whole area.[47]

Betsy Edwards's interview of Hattie covered the looming removal of people from public housing on the pretext that the CHA was going to rehab the apartments. Most of the people who were removed had no place to live when the public housing was torn down. Hattie came to some conclusions by observing the infrastructure work that was being done in the area and by her own experience with the CHA. Hattie and her interviewer discussed the proposed renovation of the housing. The questions and Hattie's answers follow.

Q. So then they could put up condos worth $300,000.

A. Two years ago at 44th and Lake Park down the street, the whole street was torn apart that year. And you should see the sewage system is so big there that a grown man could walk through it. Then they paved it all over, but I knew that something big is going to need a lot of sewage system when it is ready.

Q. Oh, you're kidding, they've already laid the sewage system?

A. Yes, and then what they did a few years back, they like to get a community leader such as myself and put me on the planning board so that they can say they consulted the community. I ended up on two planning boards. That's why I knew so much about what was going to happen. I ended up on the planning boards, but I resigned from the planning boards because I'm not going to be the rubber stamper.

Q. How do you keep from feeling hopeless?

A. I think that the philosophy that we have in Shalom here, in the mission-in-reverse philosophy is, if you give a person certain skills, they can take the skills with them. If you teach me to fish, I can fish for myself. But if you just hand me a fish

---

47 Edwards, interview, 15ff.

all the time, you are really not helping me, because I really need you to hand me that fish. I feel that the things that we have done in the past nine years at Shalom, is to teach people how to get receivership of a building, and how to organize and keep the building in good shape, and this is happening to teach the people skills like painting, plastering, how to do that kind of work.

We were able to do that to a building at 3970. Why the building is not there now is the lawyer that was appointed to act as receiver of the building for the tenants whom we had organized into a tenants council group, he fled with the money and did not pay the bills. So the $8,000 furnace was vandalized and taken out of the basement. The people said we can't face a second winter in the cold. Because the first winter that Shalom went down there, there were two nuns that lived here, and they were the ones who helped the people get organized and show them how. Goldfish were frozen in solid cakes of ice in aquariums; cats were frozen in the doorways, crouched and dead. With the people getting the victory, the sweet smell of victory, the receivership, and then to see the lawyer fade out. That was the year that Harold Washington was elected mayor [1983], by the way, and this lawyer said he had holdings in California, and he left.

…So what came out of that then? Is that a total loss? I would say no. Because the people had the means of knowing how to organize. They would know what to look for, and the young people in the buildings and in the neighborhoods were taught skills, and they were able, some of them to get some kind of handyman jobs. So that's what it leads to.[48]

Operating and maintenance costs were high during the 1970s and 1980s, and inept management added to the desperate financial situation of the CHA. The federal Department Housing and Urban Development (HUD) had deemed the CHA "troubled" as far back as 1979. Finally, in 1995 HUD took complete control of the CHA by means of an administrative receivership, meaning an employee of HUD was put in charge of the management of all the public housing in Chicago. The

---
48 Edwards, interview, 15ff.

action was based on the criteria of long-standing, severe, and persistent management problems. HUD retained that control until 1999 when it was deemed that the CHA technically was no longer troubled, albeit still not completely fixed. Many of its housing developments were still in very poor condition.

Along with lifting the receivership, HUD gave the city $1.5 million from federally funded HOPE VI (Housing Opportunities for People Everywhere)[49] funds over ten years. The money was supposed to be used to aggressively and completely remake the CHA and its mission. In 1999, when the CHA was given back to the city under Mayor Richard M Daley, a new plan, "The Plan for Transformation," was designed with the goal of remaking the CHA and its mission. Under the Plan for Transformation, the CHA would no longer be in the business of buying and renting housing units. Instead, it would serve as a facilitator for the renovation and remaking of all its developments. This was a plan of scope and scale beyond anything attempted in the whole country.

The Plan for Transformation called for demolishing 18,500 of the CHA's existing family apartments while renovating another 5,810 units, which were mostly in low-rise and mid-rise buildings. The 9,500 apartments for seniors were mainly in high-rise buildings and were to be spared demolition. Using $1.5 billion in federal HOPE VI funds, the goal was to rehabilitate the entire stock of public housing in Chicago.

Hattie had this to say about these plans:

> In this area now we're undergoing a change. This is up for redevelopment. I would say from 35th and Lake Park to 47th. We won't be here another decade from now, for the redevelopment plans, there would be upper income people that would not be black. There, higher, you know rents, redevelopments of different types of housing than you would see here now. Public housing up and down here. But several redevelopments, in another decade. Those houses like this that I'm living in, these will be condemned. It's impossible to get a loan from a local bank, to rehab, or to do anything

---

[49] HOPE VI is a plan by the United States Department of Housing and Urban Development to revitalize the worst public housing projects in the United States and turn them into mixed-income developments. The program began in 1992, with formal recognition by law in 1998.

> in your home. You can't get improvements money. It's been redlined. The whole area—you can't get any help in rehabbing through the local bank.
>
> …I've seen the tactics—how redevelopment plans come through. It's not just against blacks. I've seen whole Polish and Lithuanian neighborhoods moved out, en masse here to make room for an expressway, you know, the Stevenson, the Eisenhower. And so I don't necessarily label it as black but I know the whole mechanism of what happens, when a neighborhood is going to be redeveloped and how it's done and how the people are really duped and put out. So the projects are being cleared down.[50]

Myers asked Hattie about the plans for the housing projects.

> Well, they claim that they are going to be rehabbed, and those who qualify will be allowed to return to the lakefront. "Those who qualify." When I hear that kind of rhetoric, then I want to know what's the criteria for returning. So it's a big question there and I could be wrong. But I do not see this, as it is, the only lakefront in a slum area where you're right on Lake Michigan. This is choice land, and I just don't think we're long for this neighborhood.[51]

The renovated buildings were to feature various types of housing—townhouses, duplexes, condos, and single-family homes. To achieve the mixed-income goal, one-third of the units were to be reserved for low-income tenants. The others were rented at affordable prices and a third were rented at market rate. This sounds fair enough, but the people who were dispossessed of their homes were mainly low-income renters who could not afford the units supposedly reserved for them.

By the end of the Plan for Transformation, the CHA expected to have constructed thousands of units in mixed-income developments in neighborhoods made desirable by their nearness to the amenities of Chicago and the removal of poor, black people. Row houses that looked like other row houses in the city were to be built. It was thought that attractive

---

50 Myers, interview, 5.
51 Myers, interview, 5.

design and construction would attract working-class and market-rate families, which would remove the stigma from public housing.

The Plan for Transformation was formulated without input from tenant representatives or housing advocates. Several serious problems arose: the shrinking total of housing units available; selection of return residents; ignoring squatters who previously lived in the buildings; scattering of people who took housing vouchers but hoped to return when the apartments were ready. Still another problem was the institution of daunting new rules for returning residents. A resident applying for housing was required to spend thirty hours a week at work, school, or training. Also, tough administration and eviction policies were put in place.

Residents who were forced to move from the public housing were offered three benefits. If they were deemed "lease compliant" in their current housing, they would have the right to return when the new housing was built. They would also be offered Housing Choice Vouchers, formerly called Section 8 Housing, to pay rent for housing that was available on the market in the private sector. Also, they would be connected to the city's private and social services to receive job training, counseling, and other services as part of a "Moving to Work" initiative, a federal program.

Not surprisingly, there is a waitlist for moving into the new housing for people who were evicted from the old housing. When a family applies for housing in the new mixed-income housing, their name is placed in a lottery. Names drawn from the lottery are put on the family Waitlist. When a unit becomes available, the family will be contacted and screened according to housing needs and family size. After that screening, they will be declared either eligible or ineligible to rent a unit. Thus, a family has to apply to be put on a Waitlist and then must wait for a lottery to be held, at which time their name may or may not be drawn.

Between October 27 and November 24, 2014, the CHA opened registration for the 2015 Waitlist Lottery. During that time 282,000 households applied which, according to the CHA website, was the largest number in Waitlist history. With only 40,000 available vouchers, the lottery was held in April 2015. Based on the results of that lottery, names were randomly selected to be placed on the following Waitlists: Family Public Housing, Housing Choice Voucher, and Property Rental Assistance.

In late April 2015, notification letters with the results of the Waitlist Lottery were sent to all registrants who provided a valid mailing address. Registrants were informed that the estimated wait time before being contacted to be screened for a housing opportunity was expected to be one to five years. This was after they had waited years to be selected, even to be considered for application. What does a family do in the meantime? The CHA suggests that people who are waiting investigate resources offered by the city of Chicago or affordable rental opportunities at the state of Illinois website or through partner organization Access Living, which advocates for housing for disabled people.

As public housing was torn down and replaced with a variety of home designs, the property values of remaining homes and newly constructed homes increased. When we knew Hattie, her home was worth about $20,000. The last time her house was sold was in 2011, for $62,500.

Now the high-rises are gone, replaced by private homes, condos, and apartment buildings. Parks and avenues connect new homes and thriving businesses. Common sense says this is a good thing, but the burning question is where have all the people gone? In 1980, Hattie told us that in ten years all the people would be gone, driven to other places and conditions of poverty.

Chapter 7
BABIES HAVING BABIES

Hattie was both angered and grieved by the extensiveness of teenage pregnancy in Bronzeville. She called it "babies having babies." What she saw as she went among the people were little girls, eleven, twelve, thirteen years old getting pregnant, giving birth, and struggling to be mothers.

She was a regular visitor in the public housing buildings in Bronzeville where many of the young mothers lived with their families. Sometimes she went in response to emergency calls for help. Sometimes she took food and clothing and furniture to families she knew were having a hard time living from day to day. Sometimes she attended resident meetings and protests. Sometimes she went just to visit friends. Sometimes she went to invite people to her home for the various activities she organized.

It was this last instance that served as the setting for an article she wrote for the *Chicago Sun-Times* in August 1978.[52] She had visited an apartment to invite the woman who lived there to join a community discussion group. She doesn't write what the topic of the group was to be, but it could have been on a wide range of topics from good parenting skills to cleaning up the debris-strewn empty lots to the state of education in the neighborhood schools.

She wrote that whenever she walked into an apartment in the public housing buildings she never knew what she would see. One day she "came upon a scene that I can't get out of my mind." As she walked up to the door of the apartment she wanted to visit, she saw that it was slightly open. She called out the name of the woman who lived there and identified herself. A ten-year-old girl "with a vacant stare" told her to come in. She said that her mother was asleep and her big sister was in the back bedroom.

---

52 Hattie Kay Williams, "The Children of God in Apartment X," *Chicago Sun-Times* (August 30, 1978), 69. See also Hattie Kay Williams, "Urban Epidemic: Babies Having Babies," *Chicago Sun-Times* (August 29, 1978), 37. These were a two-part series in the View section of the *Sun-Times*.

As Hattie entered the apartment the smell of urine and dirty clothes filled her nostrils. As her eyes adjusted to the semi-darkness of the small room, she saw two babies. Both were naked except for wet, soggy diapers. Both had frail, thin bodies with "large navels protruding from swollen stomachs." One of the babies who was about six months old was crying faintly. The other baby was an eighteen-month-old who "was quietly rocking on his knees and bumping his head on the wall. A dark round callous had formed on his little forehead."

The little girl who opened the door for Hattie ran into the bedroom to awaken her mother. As she reported that her mother would be right out, the other bedroom door opened and a young woman of about seventeen emerged. She was clad only in a sheet. She scolded the little girl because the younger baby was crying. She ordered her to "put some more sugar water in the little --------'s bottle and you'd better shut him up."

Then she noticed Hattie and said, "Oh, hello Mrs. Williams. I didn't see you sitting there." As she opened the door to return to the bedroom, Hattie saw a young man lying on the bed in his shorts. Finally, Mrs. Greene (a fictitious name) came out of her bedroom and raised the shades. She explained that the health clinic had given her more pills to help calm her nerves. "They are really good. These kids can climb the walls and I don't even hear them when I am in my bedroom." At that point, she noticed that it was 2:30 p.m. and her ten-year-old daughter should have been in school. When she scolded her for not going to school, the little girl responded that Big Sis made her stay home to babysit.

Hattie invited Mrs. Greene to the meeting but before she left urged her to get medical help for the very visible navel ruptures in the grandbabies. Mrs. Greene said, "I'll tell my daughter about that when she gets home; she must see about that when she gets home because they're hers not mine." This is not a typical, widespread reaction of grandmothers of any race who take care of neglected children. There are untold numbers of stories of black grandmothers who sacrificed all for their grandchildren. Many grandmothers were and are virtually mothers to their children's children.

The ten-year-old girl told her mother that her big sister was in the bedroom with her boyfriend. Before Mrs. Greene could check out her daughter's room, there was a loud scream at the apartment door. In ran her thirteen-year-old daughter, "crying because two boys had pulled down her blouse, exposing her developing breasts."

As usual the elevators were out of order so as Hattie walked down the many flights of stairs she asked herself these questions:

> Are my people becoming the inferior race, we are often labeled as being? Are we trapped in the process of becoming obsolete? We were brought here as slaves, and now that we are no longer necessary in the cotton fields, are we being permitted to destroy ourselves?[53]

Hattie's observations in the article continue as she writes about one of the many problems facing black people—the availability of legal drugs ruining the minds of more black people than the illegal drugs. She wrote that the mother she just described was typical.

> Women are tranquilized and resting every day on pills prescribed by doctors who specialize in Medicaid families, while her teenagers are having sex in the house, another child is not in school half the time, the two grandchildren receive no prenatal or postnatal care, and her prescription can be refilled without medical follow-up or supervision, so she can remain in a stupor indefinitely. I have no pat answers, but I think one approach is to improve the spiritual life of people in the community. There is a great emptiness of spirit. The churches must come out of their sanctuaries and reach into the community in new, relevant ways. I am a devout Catholic, and I see it necessary for my own church to begin this outreach. We don't have social centers. We don't have recreation. The only thing the young people can do is fight or have sex. It's important, too, that we have more jobs. But first we've got to plant the seed so inner strength, spiritual strength will grow, or the young won't develop the potential a job can give them.[54]

Ten years after the publication of this article, Betsy Edwards, a close friend of Hattie, asked her if the situation of babies having babies was worse than when she wrote the article in 1978.

---

53 Williams, "Children of God in Apartment X," 69.
54 Williams, "Children of God in Apartment X," 69.

Oh, yes. Much worse than in 1978. Now everybody is aware that babies are having babies. Not only that, it has worsened to such an extent that we have birth controls dispensed in DuSable High School and other schools in the black community. I don't feel that the school should be a catch all for the evils that befall the black community. It's an educational institution. It's not doing its job so why make it a social service or medical center. I don't see the need for doing that, and the few girls who are not active sexually get a double message. You are supposed to have sex. We have the clinic here. So I feel that if you are going to go that far, then set up some cots in the gymnasium and let them go all the way. I feel that it should not be just pills, pills, pills. Our girls are not encouraged to use any other forms of contraceptives rather than the pills. They don't have a freedom of choice; that's it.

There were people who sent mail to the *Sun-Times* saying that I was right on target and agreeing. There were people who were indignant and felt that I had aired the black problem in the white press. There were people who used these articles in workshops for discussion groups, and then there were some who were really hostile enough to all but threaten me. At one time all five of my sons had to be here around this house. They felt that I was being threatened.

Q. By whom? Men?

A. Yes, males, black males who felt that I had aired this in the press.

Q. Did they feel that you had speared the black males?

A. Yes, then I had some good things happen. I had a young black social worker who said, "I had a baby at fourteen. I went back and got my Bachelor's degree, and I would like to come and talk to some of the young women and people in the neighborhood. You are telling the truth. You don't have to be that way. You can pick up the pieces of your life and you can make something worthwhile." I thought that was a worthwhile thing, and that continued for two years. This young social worker instilled a lot among some of the young women such as good grooming habits, having a better sense of self-worth about yourself, and you are somebody, how to prepare yourself for a job application, what to wear and how to dress, even deodorants. This young lady was very dedicated, and I had several young women come in to do this type of work, and coming from young black women it was good.

At Operation Push[55] they had a day for me. There was a day in my honor for being on target on this subject. But the condition, sad to say, has worsened. I feel that the black family is being undermined and destroyed.

Q. What are the forces that are doing this?

A. Well, look at it this way. I feel that it's profitable for others if blacks cannot read or write, if blacks remain on the welfare system and suppression. I will give you an idea of what I mean. Say there's a day care center in this neighborhood. Say it's located in public housing, and it is, and you go in and see how many babies there are in the day care center. No matter what time of day you go. But it's political patronage people in there, not people who are qualified in early childhood development or education. How do they keep their jobs? As long as those babies are being born. The girls say, "I want to go back to school or I want to get a job." They drop those babies off down there, where they are ill-cared for. So as long as the treadmill of babies keeps coming out, it is feasible to keep it that way. It's a grist mill, that's what I call it. That's one of the reasons that I say it's profitable for people not to be prepared when you've got a welfare rewarding system rewarding a young girl to be independent living, then the mother of that girl can't tell that girl anything.

"I'm a woman. I've performed. I've had a baby just like you had a baby, I get my own check."

---

[55] Operation PUSH (People United to Serve Humanity) was founded by the Rev. Jesse Jackson in 1971. It is a social justice organization that is now merged with the National Rainbow Coalition, a political organization Jackson founded in the 1980s.

She's still not a responsible adult. She buys Jordache blue jeans and fingernail polish with her check and she and her baby are looking at her momma. So when you've got a system like that, it breaks down the family.

Q. How young can they get their welfare checks?

A. I don't know how young. It seems like the majority are sixteen-year-old girls that get the checks. So what does that mean? The boys can't read or write, can't fill out a job application. How are they going to survive when they are eighteen and taken off their mother's welfare grant? This can happen even at twelve if they are not in school. If a youth drops out at twelve the mother don't get to feed him no more, as far as the check is concerned.

So then, where does this young man get his money from? What does he do? What he has to do. He either becomes an ADC pimp if he's old enough to be a father, gets himself two or three girlfriends and keeps them barefoot and pregnant, and takes from her and takes from her and takes from her, or robs, or he can sell drugs. That's the three choices that is open to an uneducated black male who cannot read or write. Sometimes they do all three, sometimes they figure it's much more profitable to get a bunch of girls, it's more fun, get them pregnant, don't worry about the baby. ADC takes care of them. You just know her check day and get part of her money. And if she gets wise enough to resist you… (The interview records end here.)[56]

In the *Sun-Times* article and in this interview, Hattie laid out some of the causes of teen pregnancy in the ghetto. In Hattie's deep and wide experience, the causes were lack of spirituality, family breakdown, low self-esteem, unpreparedness for the world, drugs, welfare, and sex education. All these causes are interconnected. One problem breeds another. For many girls, forces are at work which make the choice of intercourse and pregnancy the only one they think will improve their lives.

---

56 Edwards, interview, 34.

In some cases, pregnancy may have been a result of incest or rape. However, among the older teenagers, it was often a choice that each girl made. How many girls, black and white, rich and poor, have given in to the insistence of their boyfriends that "If you truly love me you will have sex with me. If you don't love me that much I will find another girl who will"?

The need to be loved often shrank to the expectation that at least a baby would love her. This reason for pregnancy is not unique to poor teenage girls in a ghetto but is common among women who need someone to love them unconditionally and absolutely. That need for love blocks out any common sense or knowledge that there is more to having a baby than just being loved by the child.

Sometimes a welfare check would be the incentive for a girl to get pregnant. If she had a baby, the reasoning was, she could get welfare which would be her own money to do with as she pleased. Seldom did a girl realize that the check would not ever be sufficient to cover all the needs she and her child would have. Even worse was if the father of her child was what Hattie called a "welfare pimp," a man or boy who had intercourse with several girls or women. The babies that resulted enabled the men to collect from the mothers each time they received a welfare check meant for the mothers and their children.

Hattie's thoughts and experiences call for more detail on welfare and on the adequacy of sex education in Chicago.

The history of welfare in the United States goes back as far as colonial times. While friends and neighbors did what they could to help families in need, public provision was also made for them. Local governments or charities administered poorhouses, almshouses, orphanages, and workhouses to accommodate and provide for very poor families. Local officials decided who went to the poorhouses and who would receive help at home. There was much discrimination as to who was "deserving" of aid. The depth of a family's poverty did not carry as much weight as did their worthiness in the eyes of the welfare officials. This is not as archaic as it sounds. Who deserves aid and why they don't is still, in the twenty-first century, a major issue in welfare legislation at the federal and state levels.

Then, as now, there existed a general prejudice against people on relief. Single mothers were in a double bind. If they applied for relief, they were often labeled by the community as morally unfit. If they worked outside the home, they were accused of neglecting their children. Even while praising "stay at home" moms, society did and still does require that poor mothers be compelled to work if they are to receive any public aid.

Early in the twentieth century, child welfare reformers, women's clubs, and juvenile court judges lobbied for mothers' pensions that prevented families from being sent to the poorhouse, forced mothers to give up their children, or made children go into the labor force. In 1909, President Theodore Roosevelt called a White House conference on how to deal with the problem of single mothers and their children. The conference declared that keeping a family together in its home was far more effective than putting them in institutions, as had been the practice in decades past.

In 1911 the Illinois State Legislature passed the first mothers' pension law in the United States. Within the next decade, forty other states followed suit. The Illinois law was titled "Funds to Parents Act" and was separate from other relief programs. It was intended to provide a subsidy to all families with dependent children who were without an adult male income. The act did not provide any funds for the support of the mothers and children but gave permission to counties to use public funds for this purpose. The application of the program was often determined by the willingness and ability of each county to come up with the needed funds.

The mothers' pension laws were meant to be a subsidy, not a replacement for earned income. Some of the states restricted the subsidy to widows, and some gave them to women whose husbands were in the hospital or in jail. Only two, Nebraska and Michigan, gave them to unmarried women. Black women, deserted and divorced women, and women with only one child did not qualify for the pension so they were directed to other programs.

The reformers lobbying for the bill maintained that much good would come from it because with financial aid mothers could stay home and watch over their children's activities. However, the subsidies were never sufficient to allow mothers to stay home. In a counterproductive way, the program required recipients to work outside the home for a certain number of hours a week. Much like the attitude of some people today towards needy women and their children, mothers who could afford to stay at home were lauded while mothers who had to work even in order to be given a subsidy were denigrated.

The Federal Children's Bureau was formed in 1912 during the presidency of William Howard Taft. Its purpose was to "investigate and report on all matters pertaining to the welfare of children and child life among all classes of our people."[57] In particular, the Bureau was charged with looking at infant mortality, the birth rate, orphanages, juvenile courts, dangerous occupations, accidents and diseases of children, and employment. That was a tall order for a small, underfunded bureau but they accomplished remarkable things on behalf of children and families. Congress only appropriated $25,140 for the first year of operation, an amount that was supposed to cover the salaries of fifteen people besides the chief.

Julia Lathrop was appointed the first chief of the Children's Bureau. As was true of many of the great reformers of the early twentieth century, Lathrop was a resident of Jane Addams's Hull House in Chicago. She was filled with the same spirit of seeking social justice as was Jane Addams. In 1890, while in Chicago, she set up the first juvenile court and a psychiatric clinic for young offenders. She had been at Hull House for twenty-two years at the time of her appointment in 1912 to be the first chief of the Children's Bureau. In that position, she made issues such as child labor laws and juvenile delinquency a high priority. The first woman to head a federal department, Lathrop labored in this position for nine years on behalf of women and children. Under her leadership and that of the chiefs who followed her, the Children's Bureau created child welfare policy and led in the implementation of that policy.

Her work led to the passage of the Sheppard-Towner Act of 1921, The Promotion of the Welfare and Hygiene of Maternity and Infancy Act. This act gave states the first federal grants for human services. Under the law, which was signed on November 23, 1921, the Children's Bureau directed matching funds to states for maternal and infant health care services. At the time childbirth was the second leading cause of death among women. 20 percent of children died in their first year. 33 percent

---

57 Children's Bureau, *The Children's Bureau Legacy: Ensuring the Right to Childhood* (Washington, DC: Children's Bureau, U.S. Department of Health & Human Services, undated), https://cb100.acf.hhs.gov/sites/default/files/cb_ebook/cb_ebook.pdf.

died before they were five. Not everyone thought it was a good law. Lathrop's critics, including the American Medical Association, called the law an "imported socialist scheme" and accused her and the other women advocates of being communist conspirators.

The services included traveling health centers, nurse home visits, midwife training and licensing, parent education, nutrition literature, and data collection. The Children's Bureau advocated for something we take totally for granted today: birth registration of each child. One of the bureau's main goals was the study of infant mortality, and it needed a means to find out where and when children were born and in what circumstances so that infant mortality could be more accurately studied.

Grace Abbott succeeded Julia Lathrop in 1921 as chief of the Children's Bureau, and she served in that capacity until 1934. The press referred to her as "Mother of America's 43 million children." Abbott, who also had been a long-term resident of Hull House, maintained that "justice for all children is the high ideal in a democracy."[58]

In its 1926 bulletin "Public Aid to Mothers With Dependent Children," the Children's Bureau summarized the history of mothers' aid laws. This history laid important groundwork for the Aid to Dependent Children section of the 1935 Social Security Act. The section was later renamed Aid to Families with Dependent Children, a title that was used for sixty-one years.

An interesting sideline in this day of unaccompanied refugee children to the United States is that the Children's Bureau took on the task of facilitating the care and safety of evacuated children. They found foster home placements for 8,000 unaccompanied European children who came to the United States during World War II. At the end of the war, the Children's Bureau also helped find homes for more than 1,000 children and displaced adolescent survivors of concentration camps. In 1961 the bureau found places for unaccompanied children from Cuba. In just two years, from December 1960 to October 1962, 14,048 children were brought to the United States from Cuba. In 1975 just before the fall of Saigon in April, 2,000 infants and children were evacuated from South

---

58 John Sorensen, "Grace Abbott: Social Work Pioneer, Reformer, Hull House Resident and Chief of The Children's Bureau," *Social Welfare History Project*, 2011, http://socialwelfare.library.vcu.edu/organizations/childrens-bureau/abbott-grace/.

Vietnam. The Agency for International Development was responsible for this effort, titled "Operation Babylift."

In October 1929, the stock market crashed, and the Great Depression began. At the onset, about eighteen million elderly people, people with disabilities, and single mothers with children were already living at a bare subsistence level. So many people were thrown out of work that state and local governments and charities could not meet their needs. Children suffered most severely. Grace Abbott, head of the federal Children's Bureau, reported that in the spring of 1933, 20 percent of the nation's schoolchildren showed evidence of poor nutrition, housing, and medical care.

The severity of the Great Depression made federal action a necessity. No other entities could cope with the growing number of people facing poverty. In 1934, the Committee on Economic Security was developing proposals for public assistance for the aged, for general public health, and unemployment compensation. The committee, appointed by President Franklin Delano Roosevelt, requested that the Children's Bureau collect data and make proposals for children's programs. The work of this committee evolved into the Social Security Act of 1935, which FDR signed into law on April 14, 1935.

Title IV of the Social Security Act deals with needy families. The Act states that the purpose of this part is

> (1) to increase the flexibility of states in operating a program designed to provide assistance to needy families so that children may be cared for in their own homes or in the homes of relatives,

> (2) to end the dependence of needy parents on government benefits by promoting job preparation, work, and marriage,

> (3) to prevent and reduce the incidence of out-of-wedlock pregnancies and establish annual numerical goals for preventing and reducing the incidence of these pregnancies, and

(4) to encourage the formation and maintenance of two-parent families.[59]

Title V was written to provide for maternal and child welfare. It was to include maternal and child health services, services for crippled children, child welfare services, and vocational rehabilitation.

Grace Abbott and Katherine Lenroot, the second and third successors to Julia Lathrop as head of the Children's Bureau, lobbied tirelessly to ensure that aid for children who would otherwise live in poverty be added to the bill. The Social Security Act was aimed at male breadwinners, reflecting the assumption of the writers of the bill that only fathers provided support for their families. The goal of Abbott and Lenroot was to get help for families who lacked a male breadwinner. Mothers' aid laws typically applied only to "deserving" women, usually married women who had been widowed or abandoned. However, to Abbott and Lenroot it made no difference how the women got into the position of being single mothers. For them it was not a moral right or wrong issue. The issue was taking care of children. Not only did they want cash stipends for needy mothers and their children, they also wanted counselors who would work with mothers to improve their skills in parenting, nutrition, budgeting, and other areas where help might be needed.

In drafting the act, the Committee on Economic Security ignored the suggestions of Abbott and Lenroot. The committee made participation by the states voluntary, which made it possible for states that placed an onus on public aid to reject the law. It also removed a provision that required the program to pay an amount of cash that was compatible with health and decency. This removal made it possible for each state to decide what constituted health and decency and how much would be paid. At the same time, the administration of the Children's Bureau was transferred to the Social Security Administration, which did not have the same commitment to poor children and their mothers. This changed the vision of the original Children's Bureau from one of being a single federal agency lobbying for the needs of all children to one focused on the needs of specific groups. Another blow to the attempt to help poor mothers and their children was that the initial appropriation was reduced from $120 million to $25 million.

---

59 Social Security Act Home, Compilation of the Social Security Laws, www.ilo.org/dyn/travail/docs/1580/Compilation of the Social...

The proposals that Abbott and Lenroot submitted to the Committee on Economic Security were designed to comply with the highest social work standards, offering personal casework services to lone mothers as well as providing cash stipends. They sought casework both because they wanted to remove recipients of Aid to Dependent Children (ADC) from the stigma of public assistance and because they believed that families headed by mothers were problematic and needed support and guidance.

A provision in the law authorized ADC assistance only to "suitable" homes. It functioned for the program's first three decades to reduce the number of eligible children. Right from the beginning, the program worked to inhibit coverage of "illegitimate" children and children of color. It is shocking that it was created primarily for white women who were not expected to work outside the home. Black mothers who were already in the workforce were not eligible to receive benefits. It was not until 1960 that Aid to Families with Dependent Children (AFDC) was expanded to include black women. The words "families with" were added to the name in 1962, partly because critics felt the program's rules discouraged marriage. Local AFDC policy frequently discontinued aid during seasons when there was a shortage of low-wage laborers, thus forcing poor mothers into such labor.

At first, ADC functioned mainly to provide federal grants to help the states maintain their mothers' aid laws, which had been passed in forty states between 1910 and 1920. For its first three decades, ADC operated much like a private charity, with its caseworkers given discretion in investigating clients, cutting off benefits to those determined to be unsuitable, and reducing benefits to those found in violation of any of ADC's myriad regulations.

AFDC, administered by the Department of Health and Human Services, was in effect from 1935 to 1996. It grew from a minor part of the Social Security system to a significant system of welfare administered by the states with federal funding. It was criticized by many who believed that the program discouraged marriage and offered incentives for women to have children and disincentives for them to work. In 1996, AFDC was replaced by the more restrictive Temporary Assistance for Needy Families (TANF) program.

In 1960, seventy-nine of every one hundred children were in need, but only thirty out of one hundred actually received assistance. In the mid-1960s, African American women responded to this lack of concern and attention to children by forming the National Welfare Rights Organization. Its primary purpose was to defend the rights of welfare recipients. Working with lawyers in community legal aid offices, recipients filed hundreds of cases challenging the administration of AFDC. The goal of these cases was to create a uniform federal standard of AFDC administration and to eliminate the most degrading eligibility requirements.

Hattie's experience with many teenage mothers was that they did indeed have babies in order to get a welfare check. She also experienced the fact that males were intimate with more than one girl in order to collect multiple welfare checks. Hattie did not mention directly if welfare was a disincentive to work, but she did point out that many of the people involved had insufficient education and no job skills.

Although numerous court challenges failed, by the mid-1970s the Supreme Court had broken new ground by striking down, on both statutory and constitutional grounds, some of the most draconian state provisions regulating AFDC. Some changes beneficial to the recipients were made, but most of the changes to AFDC during its seventy-year life worsened conditions for recipients.

The original purpose of AFDC was to allow mothers to stay home with their children, but starting in the 1960s the system was changed in various ways to push welfare mothers into the labor force. Further amendments provided tax incentives for taking jobs and cut off aid to those mothers who refused offers of "suitable" employment. A variety of "workfare" programs were attempted at both state and federal levels. For some time, many states allowed adult welfare recipients to attend school as a form of work, since education tends to reduce welfare dependency over time, but the provision was steadily squeezed out. In general, workfare was unsuccessful because the wages that most welfare recipients could earn were not adequate to raise children in safety and health.

Thousands were removed from the welfare rolls, not because they were better off but because of the rigid requirements for participation. The success of AFDC was evaluated in terms of declining welfare rolls, not in terms of declining childhood poverty. The welfare-to-work programs led to the repeal of the entire AFDC program in 1996.

Being on AFDC was not a bed of roses for the clients. It required filling out numerous forms, waiting endless hours in shabby, crowded public aid offices served by disillusioned caseworkers, and enduring home investigations and bed checks in the wee hours of the morning to make sure there wasn't a man in the mother's bed. Any change in one's situation required a visit to the welfare office, which in itself was burdensome. Still, the lure of cash of her own did draw many young girls into motherhood. They were Hattie's babies having babies.

In spite of all the stories of welfare queens who got rich on welfare, few poor people got rich and many stayed trapped in poverty. The fraud that recipients were and still are accused of were minor compared to the fraud perpetrated by some welfare officials, doctors, dentists, and storekeepers.

In order to clarify a very complicated system, the Kenwood Oakland Community Organization (KOCO) in 1966 printed and distributed a flyer titled, "Your Welfare Rights." On the flyer were questions that people wanting to be on welfare could submit to KOCO for answers and help. The flyer listed what families of various sizes could receive. An adult in a family of two could receive $30.31. A baby through five years old could receive $21.59. As family size increased, welfare payments decreased. For instance, an adult in a family of eight or more could receive $4.30 less than an adult in a family of two. A baby in a family of eight could receive $2.53 less each month.

These allowances were for food, clothing, household supplies, and personal essentials. The rent for the family would also be paid. If this adult and her child paid for electricity, she could add $3.90 and $2.10 for gas, making her monthly total $57.96. There were special allowances that could add a few more dollars to the monthly check.

The lure of the welfare check, inadequate as it was, may have drawn young girls into motherhood, but there is another cause of teenage and younger pregnancy. That was and is, in the eyes of many people, the lack of sex education. As shown vividly in the interview with Hattie, she thought the teaching of sex education in the public schools promoted sexual activity instead of decreasing it.

Whether sex education in public schools is a deterrent to teenage sexual activity or if it actually promotes it is a hotly debated topic even to this day. Some say it is not only important for children and youth to understand their sexual functioning but also to be aware of the consequences of sexual intimacy. With the prevalence of sexually transmitted diseases, sex education is a vital part of health education.

On the other side of the debate are advocates of abstinence who propose the use of virginity pledges made by individual teenagers who sign a written pledge or make a verbal promise to remain a virgin until marriage. Advocates of virginity pledges claim that such pledges have substantially lowered levels of sexual activity.

In addition to the programs of the Chicago Public Schools, The Chicago Department of Health is using a $19.7 million grant from President Obama's Teen Pregnancy Prevention Initiative to tackle the problem.[60]

I can only guess what Hattie would think of the current campaign of the Chicago Department of Public Health to discourage teenage pregnancy, and we can only speculate whether Hattie might disapprove of the lengths to which sex education in the Chicago Public Schools goes today or if in her wisdom she might approve. Any attempt to address such a serious, widespread problem as teenage pregnancy as a stand-alone issue is doomed to failure. That whole range of issues to which Hattie gave her life must also be considered: segregation, substandard education, low to no employment, overcrowded housing, poor policy making, and government graft and corruption.

---

60 Chicago Department of Public Health, Healthy Chicago, "Teen Pregnancy Prevention Initiative," Susan Eldder, Program Director, June 19, 2013. https://www.chicago.gov/content/dam/city/depts/cdph/policy_planning/Board_of_Health/BoardPresentationJune2013.pdf.

Chapter 8
PUBLIC SCHOOLS

"Stay in your place." That is what the principal of Oakenwald Elementary School said to Hattie when Hattie was elected the first black president of that school's Parent Teacher Association (PTA) in 1951. In her role as PTA president and as the mother of six children who attended this school, Hattie confronted the principal about the deplorable condition of the books and other resources that were used in the classrooms of black students. The principal simply responded, "Stay in your place. Don't make an issue of the matter. Blacks are in remedial instruction due to their lack of innate intelligence."

Never one to just sit back and feel depressed about a putdown, Hattie moved to do what she could to improve education for black children in Chicago. Her term at Oakenwald lasted from 1951 to 1953. From 1961 to 1963, she served as president of the Forestville Parent Teachers Association where she was a leader of public-school boycotts. From 1967 to 1969 she served on the Human Relations Department of the Chicago Board of Education. This positioned her to be a leader in the parent protests that arose in Chicago during the 1960s. Alongside her work in the education community, she held Graduate Equivalency Degree (GED) classes in her home for children who dropped out of school. Several nuns who lived in the area worked with her to help tutor those students. At one point, they were tutoring thirteen dropouts.

> I had a nun who was here for five years. If you only have thirteen graduates for your GED, General High School Equivalency, you might think that it isn't a big deal. But that was the changing of thirteen lives. That took a lot of individualized tutoring and instruction to pull that many people through. And sometimes if you can be a change agent for only thirteen, you never know how that's going to affect their lives. We kept up with a few of them. I don't feel helpless to this extent. I think like Mother Teresa over there in India, where you see people dying of hunger, leprosy. She says, "I am not

called to success. I'm called to serve." You won't need statistics to say how much of success I am going to be. What's the use of it? If you do that then you will suffer burnout right away. I am called to pray and to be persistent and to be patient. That's my three P's. To pray, persist, and be patient. I have to understand that I am one individual and I can't do a whole lot. But I can be a little salt, and it can spread out. I can be a little leaven and things will rise.[61]

Hattie was more than a little leaven in the story of the many attempts to integrate public schools in Chicago. The prejudice she experienced during her childhood and adolescence, as well as the segregation she faced when she worked with the parents and children in Kenwood/Oakland, was nothing new for black people in Chicago. The education of black children in Chicago has been a story of exclusion, segregation, and neglect. Local prejudice on the part of whites in Chicago was intertwined with state and federal policy which was also prejudiced concerning public education.

To go back to the Revolutionary War when talking about segregated schools in Hattie's time seems like a stretch, but that was when the groundwork for public education in the United States was laid. Control of the Northwest Territory passed from Great Britain to the Confederation of the United States in the Treaty of Paris in 1783, which ended the Revolutionary War. The Northwest Territory was an expanse of land that included the area that was to become the states of Indiana, Ohio, Illinois, Michigan, Wisconsin, and Minnesota. A major issue with this acquisition was how to organize and govern 170 million acres of forest that had hardly been touched, prairies that had not been plowed, waterways that were pristine.

This history is relevant in a discussion of public education in Hattie's day and even today because it displays the strongly held belief of the founders of our country of the necessity of public education. It remains of great importance today as more and more people seek private education for their children, white and black, thus endangering the provision of an equal education for all children. On May 20, 1785, the Congress of the Confederation adopted a standard system for selling and settling the land of this vast territory. The whole Northwest Territory was to be di-

---

61 Edwards, interview, 16.

vided for sale into townships six-miles square. Each township would be subdivided into lots one-mile square, 640 acres, and numbered from one to thirty-six. Recognizing the value of public education, the Congress decreed that Lot Number 16 in each township was to be reserved for the maintenance of public schools. Congress would give ownership of the Section 16 lots to be used or sold with the stipulation that all the money raised from that land would go into a school fund to build and maintain public schools. Illinois received 985,066 acres of Section 16 lands.

The Ordinance urged the new states to make provisions for public education and to prohibit slavery within their borders. Article 3 declared, "Religion, morality, and knowledge being necessary to good government and the happiness of mankind, schools and the means of education shall forever be encouraged." Article 6 laid down an absolute prohibition: "There shall be neither Slavery nor involuntary Servitude in the said territory." On August 7, 1789, President George Washington signed a replacement, the Northwest Ordinance of 1789, in which the new United States Congress reaffirmed the original ordinance with slight modifications under the newly effective Constitution of the United States.

Illinois became a state in 1818, and its first act for establishing public education was passed in 1825. This act, titled the Free School Law, stated that public schools would be open and free to every class of white student between the ages of five and twenty-one. Later revisions changed the discriminatory language of the first section of the law but kept language that implied the term "white" in regard to administration and sharing of funds for education. The privilege of an education in Illinois was clearly reserved for white children.

Chicago was incorporated in 1833 having reached a population of three hundred. The city enacted its first public school law in 1835. Like the state, it provided for education for white children only. The state was to pay for the education of white children, but payment for the few black children who were able to attend had to arranged for by other means.

In 1847, with an increase of population in Illinois, a constitutional convention was held in order to meet demands to revise and amend the Illinois constitution of 1818. During this convention, an education article was prepared as part of the new constitution. A majority of the delegates voted against it because they feared it would bring black children into white schools. One of the arguments against integrated classrooms was that having the children share classrooms and play together on the playgrounds might lead to racial "amalgamation," or, in other words, mixed marriages. Mixed marriage, although disguised by other excuses, has always been a major fear for segregationists.

Two laws that enforced discrimination against black people were the Fugitive Slave Act of 1850, passed by Congress, and the 1853 Illinois Black Code, passed by the Illinois state legislature. The Fugitive Slave Act mandated the return of escaped slaves to their owners regardless of where the slaves were captured. This law prevented runaway slaves from settling legally in free states and provided an impetus for the growth of Underground Railroad routes through free states such as Illinois.

The Illinois Black Code of 1853 prohibited any black persons from outside the state from staying in the state for more than ten days. Possible penalties were arrest, detention, a fifty-dollar fine, deportation, or being sold at public auction. Such laws were seldom enforced, but to black people they served as threatening reminders of the intention of whites to legally oppress them. These laws offered white authorities and mobs excuses for harassment and violence against blacks.

A fascinating, powerful phrase used by Zebina Eastman in an article he wrote in 1883 about the Black Code is "permission under prohibition."[62] Eastman used the phrase as he described the Black Code in a booklet by that name. In his published articles, speeches, and newspapers, Eastman was a strong and persistent voice for the anti-slavery movement in Chicago. In this booklet he outlined the way various laws give "permission under prohibition." For instance, the Black Code decreed that no one could be made a servant unless they did so out of their own free will. That is the prohibition. The permission is that a person could be made a slave if they agreed to it. Few would agree to such a thing but the people who did the enslaving could say that it was done with the person's permission. This kind of crafty evasion of laws regarding the equality of blacks persisted even under the *Brown v. Board of Education* ruling, which came almost one hundred years later.

---

62 Zebina Eastman, *Black Code of Illinois* (Chicago: 1883), 19.

The issue of segregated schools in Chicago was decided by the passage of what was called the Black School Law.

> Under the Consolidation Act for Chicago Ordinances which took effect on February 13, 1863, schools in the city were to be segregated. The part of that act which related to schools for blacks read, 'It shall be the duty of the common council and board of education to provide one or more schools for the instruction of negro and mulatto children, to be kept in a separate building to be provided for that purpose, at which colored pupils, between the ages of five and twenty-one years, residing in any school district in said city, shall be allowed to attend; and hereafter it shall not be lawful for such pupils to attend any public schools in the city of Chicago, at which white children are taught, after a school for the instruction of negro and mulatto children has been provided.' Document 42 conformed with state law and stipulated that the school for blacks would be in the South Division where a majority of black Chicago residents lived. Although most Chicago citizens opposed slavery, black freedom, but not equality, was the prevalent sentiment.[63]

Illinois repealed the "Black Code" laws following the Civil War in 1865, the same year the US Congress ended the legal institution of slavery with the passage of the 13th Amendment. To help ensure the rights of newly freed slaves, the 14th Amendment was passed in 1868. This amendment provided for equal protection under the law and allowed Congress to enforce the amendment with appropriate legislation as long as it did not contradict the judgment of the Supreme Court.

The debate over education for black children persisted through the rest of the nineteenth century with racist advocates still seeking segregation in all the schools. In 1885, the state of Illinois passed a Civil Rights Act which prohibited discrimination in public facilities and places such as hotels, railroads, theaters, and restaurants, but the political powers in Chicago ignored this law. Blacks could not live outside a black enclave,

---

63 Document 42, Order of the Committee on Schools Providing for Segregation, March 23, 1863, Illinois State Archives, Early Chicago 1833-1871; http://www.cyberdriveillinois.com/departments/archives/teaching_packages/early_chicago/doc42.html.

theaters were allowed to seat blacks only in balconies, and restaurants were allowed to deny them admittance.

When Hattie's parents moved to Chicago as part of the vanguard of the First Great Migration, they and others on the move sought not only economic security but also a good education for their children. Along with the dream of education for their children, many of them hoped for an education for themselves via night school classes. When the first of these migrants arrived in Chicago, they found that even the worst of Chicago's schools were better than the schools they had left behind. Many southern counties provided no funding for black schools. Consequently, schools for black children were held in whatever kind of building the local blacks could afford to build or in any building that was vacant. The teacher-to-student ratio could be as low as one teacher to 125 students.

Chicago is a prime example that public education and real estate are inextricably linked anywhere in the world to this day. Where people have money to buy nice homes on prime property there are good schools for their children whether they be public or private schools. In the face of the influx of thousands of blacks, the professional realtors in Chicago debated how they should handle the situation since most whites did not want blacks for neighbors. At a meeting of the Chicago Real Estate Board in 1917, the question of the invasion of white areas by blacks was raised. As a result, the realtors appointed a Special Committee on Negro Housing whose task was to make recommendations for meeting what the realtors and citizens of Chicago saw as a looming threat.

> The stated purpose of this Special Committee was to devise a method to house and school blacks that was "feasible, practical, and humane." They adopted the following policy. Inasmuch as more territory [for black people] must be provided, it is desired in the interest of all, that each block shall be filled solidly and that further expansion shall be confined to contiguous blocks, and that the present method of obtaining a single building in scattered blocks, be discontinued.[64]

In other words, only blacks could live on a block and all the blocks where blacks lived must border on each other. This resolution affected the hous-

---

64 Alan B. Anderson and George W. Pickering, *Confronting the Color Line: The Broken Promise of the Civil Rights Movement in Chicago* (Athens, GA: The University of Georgia Press, 2007), 46.

ing market and schools not only in Chicago, where the practice of block-by-block concentration and expansion of the black population became an absolute rule, but in other American cities whose real estate boards looked to the Chicago Real Estate Board for leadership and advice.

The Real Estate Board's defense of this policy was that when blacks moved into a neighborhood property values fell. Their estimate was that the value of properties fell from 30 to 60 percent the minute the first family of color moved into a white neighborhood or when it was even rumored that a black family was moving in. The board maintained that unregulated scattered sales and leases put an undue burden on the property owner whose life savings were invested in his house. The board claimed that the public also suffered because as the property values declined so did the amount of taxes collected. Thus, the board purported to speak in "an unprejudiced spirit" by stating that both the public good and individual interests would be served by the policy of block-by- block expansion of black housing.

The realtors may have sincerely believed the claims they were making were true, but it is not coincidental that these claims produced an alliance of moral conviction with financial interest. The proclamation that segregation was good for everyone was a moral conviction. The opportunity to make money was a happy by-product of this moral stance. Realtors made money by charging higher prices to blacks who wanted to buy property and whose choice of housing was limited by this policy. At the same time, they offered lower prices to the whites who wanted to sell their houses. Not only did the realtors uphold this proclamation, they actively mobilized white fears by recommending that their members encourage white homeowners in each block to form societies for the purpose of mutual defense.[65]

In 1935, eighteen years after the ruling of the realtors in Chicago, the Neighborhood Composition Rule was put in place by Harold Ickes, the Secretary of the Interior under President Franklin Delano Roosevelt. The rule stated that public housing projects could not alter the existing racial composition of their neighborhoods. Thus, the Neighborhood Composition Rule determined that the student population in a black area would be black children and the student population in a white area would be white children. The end result was a deepening of the racism that tainted

---

65 Anderson and Pickering, *Confronting the Color Line*, 36.

Chicago. With these actions of the Chicago Real Estate Board and the Roosevelt administration, the segregation in housing resulted in segregation in public schools and became public policy.

Conditions in housing and in schools in Chicago continued to deteriorate as the black population increased rapidly during the Second Great Migration. The confluence of two events—World War II and mechanical cotton pickers—caused more people, black and white, to move from the South to Northern cities. Preparations for World War II created new jobs for both whites and blacks in the defense industry and in the conversion of peacetime industries to war production, just as it had during the World War I era. At the same time, the use of greatly improved mechanical cotton pickers forced another wave of black agricultural workers out of the South. Between 1940 and 1960, Chicago's black population grew from 278,000 to 813,000.[66]

In 1954 a major change in the interpretation of who should be educated and where occurred. The words "*Brown v. Board of Education of Topeka*" are part of the memory and vocabulary of Americans. This case, brought by a black parent in Topeka, Kansas, took on segregation within school systems. Up until this case, many states had laws establishing separate schools for white students and for black students. This landmark case made those laws unconstitutional.

The decision was handed down by the United States Supreme Court on May 17, 1954. It overturned the *Plessy v. Ferguson* decision of 1896. The chief justice in the Brown case was Earl Warren, fourteenth Chief Justice of the United States. Following the unanimous 9-0 decision, Chief Justice Warren delivered the opinion of the Court:

> We conclude that, in the field of public education, the doctrine of "separate but equal" has no place. Separate educational facilities are inherently unequal. Therefore, we hold that the plaintiffs and others similarly situated for whom the actions have been brought are, by reason of the segregation complained of, deprived of the equal protection of the laws guaranteed by the Fourteenth Amendment.[67]

---

66 Manning, "African Americans."
67 *Brown v. Board*, 347 U.S. 483 (1954).

It was widely hoped and believed that the problem of segregation in public schools was settled for the nation with this decision. As important and far reaching as this decision has been, cities and their school boards have found ways around it. Zebina Eastman's phrase "prohibition with permission" held true seventy years later. Northern schools sidestepped *Brown* by claiming that their schools were segregated because of the Neighborhood Composition Rule, which in essence required blacks to live in black areas and whites to live in white areas. The result was that children who lived within walking distance of their school had to attend segregated schools.

In 1959, the US Commission on Civil Rights labeled Chicago the most residentially segregated large city in the nation.[68] Residential segregation results in educational segregation. Because of the arrival of so many people who were only allowed to live within the confines of the Black Belt, the schools for black children were severely overcrowded. In the late 1950s, schools with majority white students had an average of seven hundred students. Schools that were 90 percent black averaged an enrollment of 1,200 students. Not only were black schools overcrowded, they were supplied with inferior resources or no resources at all. The school buildings themselves were falling apart. One teacher in the 1960s reported outdated and badly used books, broken windows, torn window shades, and broken desktops. These conditions encouraged failure and a sense of depression among children, parents, and teachers.

Hattie was angry and frustrated that the schools in her neighborhood were so poorly equipped that they didn't even have libraries. Libraries of any kind in her neighborhood were in such short supply that she set one up in the basement of her home, which also contained clothing and food donations for her neighbors. Besides being director of the library, she was also the director of an after-school tutoring program, which was held daily at the Oakland Center in the Oakenwald Elementary School across the street from her home.

One of Hattie's gifts was the ability to make connections across cultural divides. For example, a B'nai B'rith Lodge had a book donation drive in the Prairie Shores apartments in July 1965, which produced several carloads of what the *Chicago Tribune* described as "old mystery stories,

---

68 Anderson and Pickering, *Confronting the Color Line*, 80.

musty text books, and last year's magazines."[69] Hattie always accepted gifts graciously, but it had to be in the back of her mind that black children deserved better!

The story of Hattie's involvement with public education in Chicago can best be told in the stories of the series of superintendents of the Chicago Public Schools during Hattie's activist days. The superintendents involved were Benjamin Willis (1953-1966), Dr. James F. Redmond (1966-1975), Dr. Joseph P. Hannon (1975-1979), and Dr. Ruth Love (1980-1985). The unalterable racist position of Superintendent Willis regarding segregation in the schools made his term the most turbulent of them all and the one in which Hattie was most involved.

While the Southern Civil Rights movement was dominating the national news, there was another movement happening that received little national coverage: the Chicago Freedom Movement for equality in public education. Hattie was a leader in this movement.

The year before the *Brown v. Board of Education* decision, Benjamin Willis, an educator with a doctorate from Columbia University, was hired to be the general superintendent of Chicago Public Schools. Some people regarded him as a pioneer in public education while others saw him as a segregationist who believed unshakably in the Neighborhood Composition Rule. His thirteen years' tenure was marked with heated controversy, boycotts, and protests fueled by the anger of black parents and many white individuals and organizations. Proponents of segregated schools not only supported Willis but also bombarded the superintendent with their complaints.

White flight from Chicago neighborhoods after World War II caused, in one generation, a third of the city's neighborhoods to go from majority white to majority black. Since the law mandated that students had to attend schools in their neighborhoods, there was little integration in the schools.

It was not an option for black parents to transfer their children to a white school where there was empty classroom space. However, a black student could transfer to a black school that was slightly less crowded. The disparity in the use of classroom space was aggravated as the black

---

[69] "Lodge Collects Library Books," *Chicago Tribune*, July 11, 1965, SCL2.

population increased and the white population decreased. Population in black areas increased because those were the only places black people could live. White schools in predominantly black areas of the city had a declining population of students because white people were fleeing to the suburbs.

In the face of charges of segregation, the Board of Education refused to survey the student body of the Chicago Public Schools to determine the number of black and white students. Finally, in the fall of 1961, the Board of Education authorized the first survey of the city's school system in thirty years. Dr. Robert Havighurst was chosen to direct the survey even though he was known as an outspoken critic of the Chicago school system. He had advocated a regional high school plan that challenged the neighborhood school concept so resolutely defended by the school administration.[70]

Havighurst's 502-page report was issued in 1964.[71] It contained three principal recommendations which would have increased the school board budget by $51.5 million a year. The report called for a major program to integrate the Chicago public schools, to improve the schools, and to encourage integration in the neighborhoods.

Portable Unit School Site, Sept 3, 1963, *Sun-Times*. Photo credit: Mann. Used by permission: *Chicago Sun-Times*.

Willis and the Board of Education steadfastly maintained that the problem of inferior education for black children had nothing to do with segregation. Rather, they said, the problem was overcrowding. They implemented two remedies that were in accordance with that stance: one for half-day shifts and another for mobile classrooms.

Since the black schools were overcrowded, black children were subjected to a schedule in which a whole school day of learning was crammed into a half day. Black students constituted only 30 percent of the citywide

---

70 John E. Coons, *Affirmative Integration: Chicago, Law & Society Review* 80 (1967), https://scholarship.law.berkeley.edu/facpubs/1996/.

student body, but they were 81 percent of the students forced to go to school in shifts.[72] Hattie's children were part of that 81 percent.

The school board's other action was to install mobile classrooms on the playgrounds of the overcrowded schools. In one case, they parked the classrooms on an empty lot near an old factory.

In January 1960, hundreds of black students were forced to move to a new school building because of overcrowding in their current schools. An abandoned warehouse located in an industrial area surrounded by railroad tracks became the new school. Black parents described it as a fire trap because it had wooden floors and staircases and no sprinkler system. In response, one board member claimed that it was fire resistant and was approved by the city of Chicago Building Department.

Hattie was one of the leaders of a group of parents and activists from many organizations and churches who banded together to boycott the classes being held in the building they called the "Willis Warehouse." The first week of February, more than two hundred of the seven hundred students stayed home from school. After five days of the boycott, Superintendent Willis decided to close the school while conditions were investigated. School officials blamed outsiders for the boycott, claiming that local parents and activists were not capable of organizing such an effective boycott on their own.

In response to the superintendent's intransigence, the parents decided on a course of action they named Operation Transfer. They applied to have their children transferred from overcrowded black schools to underutilized white schools. It was a plan to demonstrate that segregation, not overcrowding, was the problem with the schools. At the opening of the school year in 1961, one hundred and sixty parents were denied requests for transfers for their children. They knew when they asked for transfers that they would be denied but their ultimate goal was to bring a class action suit against Chicago public schools for maintaining segregated schools.

---

72 Keeanga-Yamahtta Taylor, "Challenging Jim Crow Schools in Chicago," Socialist Worker.org (February 22, 2012), http://socialistworker.org/2012/02/22/jim-crow-schools-in-Chicago,-February 22, 2012.

On September 18, 1961, this group of black parents filed suit against the Chicago Board of Education in the United States District Court for the Northern District of Illinois. The plaintiffs in *Webb v. Board of Education*, as the case was known, charged that the Board of Education maintained a deliberate policy of segregation in violation of the 14th Amendment. The plaintiffs sought to put an end to the Neighborhood Composition Rule, to stop the practice of leaving classrooms empty in white schools and end the practice of gerrymandering district boundaries to maintain racial segregation in the public schools.

Standing firm on his position that overcrowding caused the problem, in December 1961 Superintendent Willis and the Board of Education proceeded to buy 150-200 aluminum mobile school units and install them on vacant lots or on the grounds of overcrowded black schools, which in several cases eliminated playground space. The portable units were purchased with the express purpose of reducing the double shift in crowded black schools. The units, dubbed "Willis Wagons," were portable aluminum rooms approximately forty feet by twenty feet equipped with washrooms, a water fountain, electric heating, and air conditioning. They were designed to serve thirty pupils.

Representatives from a variety of Chicago organizations attended a citywide seminar, "How to Achieve Quality and Equality of Education in the Chicago Public Schools," sponsored by the Chicago Urban League and a committee of Parent Teacher Association leaders, in April 1962. The result was the formation of a coalition called the Coordinating Council of Community Organizations (CCCO). This organization was to prove powerful in the movement to improve schools in black areas. Some of the groups that made up the coalition were the Chicago Congress of Racial Equality (CORE), the Chicago Area Friends of the Student Nonviolent Coordinating Committee (SNCC), the American Friends Society, the Catholic Interracial Council, the National Association for the Advancement of Colored People (NAACP), the Presbyterian Interracial Council, and the Dearborn Real Estate Board. This coalition, in which Hattie was active, proposed a "Freedom Movement" in housing, jobs, and education for blacks in Chicago.

The *Webb v. Board of Education* case was dismissed by the judge of the district court on July 31, 1962, because he said that the plaintiffs had not exhausted all the remedies that were available at the state level and thus could not file a suit in federal court. In the face of that decision, another group of parents brought another suit, *Burroughs v. Board of Education*, in January 1962. The judge in this case also dismissed it for the same reason: the plaintiffs had not exhausted state-level remedies.

The attorneys in the *Webb* case appealed to the Supreme Court which on June 28, 1963, almost a year after the second dismissal, decided that the plaintiffs did *not* have to exhaust state level remedies in order to file in federal court. The plaintiffs reopened the case, but they ultimately settled out of court on August 29, 1963. In the settlement, the Board of Education agreed to three actions: eliminating inequities in the school system, appointing a panel to work out ways to achieve the first goal, and promising to produce a racial headcount of its pupils. They also passed a limited transfer plan that would allow the top 5 percent of students in high schools without honor courses to transfer to schools that had honors programs.

Even though the Havighurst panel set up by the Board of Education was already at work, the court ordered that another panel be formed to advise the Board on ways to eliminate inequities in the school system. This panel was composed of educators from around the country and was headed by Philip Hauser, a sociologist at the University of Chicago.[73] It began its work in September 1963, and its report was presented to the Board on March 3, 1964. However, the panel had no power to implement the changes they found were necessary to solve the problem.

Their experiences with the courts convinced the black parents that it was to no avail to resort to the legal justice system. The out-of-court settlement seemed promising only because it forced the Board of Education to acknowledge that the schools were segregated. The transfer plan was so limited that it did not even make a dent in the ability of black students to transfer to white schools.

The conflict between black activists and the school board in Chicago was happening at the same time that Governor George C. Wallace of Alabama was taking action against the integration of schools in Huntsville, Alabama. Two articles appeared on the same page of the *Chicago Daily News* on June 6, 1963. One was an account of twelve college stu-

---

73 Chicago (Ill.). Advisory Panel on Integration of the Public Schools, *Integration of the Public Schools, Chicago Report to the Board of Education* (Chicago: 1964?).

dent activists being arrested in Chicago for boycotting a school where mobile units were being installed.[74] The other pictured Alabama armed troopers surrounding schools where black parents were trying to register their children for the school year. Nationwide, the news from Alabama eclipsed the news from Chicago.

On July 10, 1963, the Council on Racial Equality (CORE) began a sit-in at the Board of Education building which lasted for eight days. Ten demonstrators, who stayed in the outer office of the President of the Board, Clair Roddewig, were removed, and eight were arrested. During the sit-in, Roddewig met with leaders from the Urban League and CORE. Roddewig announced that together they had formulated a memorandum which stated that the demonstrators would leave and that Roddewig would call a meeting of school administration officials, any school board members who wanted to attend, and CORE leaders for July 24 to hear CORE's allegations that Chicago schools were segregated.

On August 15, 1963, the *Chicago Defender* published a statement listing accusations against Superintendent Willis. It faulted him for perpetuating racial segregation in the public schools of Chicago through the use of mobile classrooms and of gerrymandering school districts for the primary purpose of keeping black children in predominately black schools. It charged him with contemptuously ignoring valid complaints of both black and white parents who believed his attitude failed to inspire confidence in the Board of Education and in the superintendent himself.[75]

The national March on Washington on August 28, 1963, became a venue for black activists from Chicago. Three thousand black and white Chicagoans attended the march and took their message of segregation in the Chicago Public Schools with them. Along with two hundred and fifty thousand people attending the March, they heard Martin Luther King Jr. give his "I Have a Dream" speech. During the march, they strode down Pennsylvania Avenue chanting "Down with Willis."

---

74 See "Wallace's Troopers Ring 4 Schools, Block Students," and "12 Arrested in School Protest," *Chicago Daily News*, June 6, 1963, 1ff.
75 "WE ACCUSE! Benjamin C. Willis," *Chicago Defender*, August 15, 1963, 1.

Demonstrations and boycotts continued in Chicago. At the Forrestville North Upper Grade Center approximately sixty mothers and children picketed peacefully at the school on September 4. They then staged a walk-in at the Board of Education offices. They were objecting to the establishment of a ninth-grade branch of DuSable High School at Forrestville, contending that facilities were inadequate. Hattie, as president of the Oakland-Kenwood-Grand Avenue Boulevard Emergency Schools Committee, was their spokesperson. She charged that the facilities at the Forrestville School were inadequate for the students. She stated that the demonstrators would resume their walk-in on September 5 and would open a "freedom school" beginning on September 16 in Ebenezer Church. She added that the freedom school would offer two hours of remedial instruction each day for students who boycotted the public schools and for students who were forced to attend substandard schools.

Hattie in Lunchroom Signing Up Children for School, September 5, 1963. Used by permission: Chicago History Museum.

Hattie confessed in an interview that she stole reading scores out of the school where she was PTA president to prove the claims of inferior education for black children.

> I was involved as a grassroots person. I was the PTA president of a local school. I stole the reading scores out of the school, turned them over to the Urban League and to CCCO [Coordinating Council of Community Organizations]. I also met with all of the parents who had children not only in the 1963 graduating class, but also in the seventh and eighth grade of this Forrestville Upper Grades Center. Those figures were so closely guarded in those days, along with the telephone numbers of any school that was not public knowledge. A parent could not call the school in an emergency or anything. That was one of the things—well, that was a diligent fight on the part of a lot of the parents in the areas that I sort of lead the fight as president of the PTA. But the figures I gave were "Exhibit A" in getting rid of Dr. Benjamin C. Willis.

Achievement level of the class of over 350 some odd youngsters and the median reading score was fifth grade down to something like two—point. [Second grade] Once I had access to them. What I did is try to communicate to other parents: "This is the condition in which our children are leaving the school going to high school, and a sort of dumping ground—I considered our local high schools dumping grounds for low achievers. That they could not possibly really achieve because of the low achievement levels when they arrived there. So that to me is like a dumping ground.[76]

The interviewer asked Hattie how she managed to steal those scores and the desperation that led her to do it.

I did it in a way when I was president of Southeast Council—that's 41 schools in this geographical area. Most of them elementary schools in Hyde Park and down here were under the jurisdiction of the Southeast Council—this is voluntary, it has nothing to do with the Board of Education. See, there are strong women, in those days there were strong women during the days of the Civil Rights movement in Hyde Park.

I don't think that I would've been able to steal all the achievement scores out of Forrestville Upper Grade Center if I had not been a very familiar face around there, to such an extent that I kept in contact with the eight feeder schools—the PTA people that were there—we had our meeting there. We had eight feeder schools, so I had a base of power you would say. So I had an office in the school, as a volunteer. So that gave me access to be there on any occasion that I wanted. And so I did that and I don't feel that was a sinful thing for me to do at the time. I was desperate. I wanted proof. I had been one of the people that had been constantly down through the years, going down to the Board of Education. They were located in one building on LaSalle 123 N. LaSalle Bank and at the hearings. They would give such a hard time to you. This is what would happen if you were going to the board for the budget hearing before the monies could be allocated to every school there was a hearing. Many times

---

76 Myers, interview, 21.

> in the black communities we're not made aware of the dates we are not vocal, we do not say what's going on or what we need for schools. So I made it a point to have workshops. And at one time I was juvenile protection of the Chicago region, Illinois Congress of parents and teachers, so I had access to giving workshops to enlighten people and to go to these budget hearings.
>
> We had a lot of support from the teachers, but it was not an outward show of support because it would've meant their jobs if they didn't have tenure or something. So we were greatly encouraged [to] fight for what we called "quality education." And we were greatly encouraged.[77]

Sit-ins and demonstrations at the offices of the Board of Education became so annoying to officials that they had a wall built in front of the stairs leading to the Board office to prevent further sit-ins. Not surprisingly, it was called the "Willis Wall."

In August 1963, a protest was held at 73rd Street and Lowe in Englewood at a site near the railroad tracks where the Chicago Board of Education was installing "Willis Wagons," aluminum trailer classrooms. As always, Superintendent Willis denied any charges of segregation, saying that the mobile units were a temporary solution to overcrowding. He asserted that they would be used only until new school buildings could be constructed.

Protestors picketed and people covered the area with all sorts of garbage and refuse. Police and protestors clashed, and four people, including both police and citizens, suffered injuries. Comedian/activist Dick Gregory was arrested for disorderly conduct during this protest.

Willis responded to these demonstrations by saying he would decide how to deal with a boycott of classes when he saw what was going to happen. He warned that it was time the parents learned that their children needed to be in class from the very first day of school. He was quoted in the *Chicago Sun-Times* as saying that he couldn't understand why there was such opposition to the units, and that he believed that "the voices of right-thinking people will win out." He maintained that the advantage

---

77 Myers, interview, 24.

of the mobile units was that they could be moved to various parts of the city as population shifts demanded.⁷⁸ Willis agreed to move mobile classrooms from one location to another in response to the demonstrations and protests, but that only spawned more demonstrations.

"**Negro Children Stage a Sitdown Protest Against Installation of Mobile Classrooms at Guggenheim School,**" August 3, 1963, *Sun-Times*. Photo credit: Jack Lenahan. Used by permission: *Chicago Sun-Times*.

As president of the Oakland Kenwood Grand Boulevard School Committee, Hattie was the spokesperson for a group of parents who staged a boycott at Guggenheim School. The parents charged that the mobile units were being used to maintain de facto segregation because the Wentworth and Guggenheim student bodies were virtually all black. They wanted the children who attended classes in mobile units to be reassigned to neighboring schools in all white or integrated areas where they claimed there was space for them.

Twenty children and an equal number of parents demonstrated at the Guggenheim school where three mobile units were in the schoolyard ready to be installed. The *Chicago Tribune* reported on the demonstration.

> Approximately 20 youngsters and an equal number of parents joined in yesterday's demonstration at Guggenheim, where three mobile units were in the school yard on blocks, ready to be installed. The youngsters lay down beneath the classrooms and were hauled away by police. Later, they returned and staged a sitdown in the school yard.
>
> While police were carrying off the youngsters, two demonstrators chained themselves to the bumpers of a squad car and a police wagon. Policemen cut them free with wire clippers and charged them with obstructing police and disorderly conduct.⁷⁹

---

78 Ronald G. Berquist, "Superintendent Amazed at Mobile Unit Protest," *Chicago Sun-Times*, August 16, 1963, 3.
79 "Seek Boycott of School: Negro Parents Want Removal of Mobile Units," *Chicago Tribune*, September 4, 1963, 1.

White parents who were against integration also organized demonstrations. A proposal to institute the transfer plan required by the out-of-court settlement of *Webb v. Board of Education* was met with strong opposition from white parents. On September 9, seven hundred white parents protested the transfer plan that would allow black students to transfer to Bogan High School, where their children were students. The next day approximately two thousand five hundred white parents met with their alderman, and on September 11 they met with Willis. Willis had ignored pressure from black parents but paid attention to the pressure from the white parents. There were twenty-four schools with honor programs that the board had said should receive transfer students who were black; Willis removed fifteen of them from the list, including Bogan High School. The Illinois State Court ordered Willis to implement a student transfer plan to bring a small number of black students to Bogan High School.

Amidst the heated controversy between pro-Willis and anti-Willis forces, Willis submitted his resignation on October 4, 1963, with two years remaining in his term. He maintained that the Board had overstepped its boundaries by making administrative decisions when its duty was to make policy decisions. Willis had powerful supporters among Chicago's most important businessmen and by prominent associations, colleges, and secondary schools, and the Board did not accept his resignation.

On October 13, 1963, the Chicago Board of Education, for the first time in its history adopted a policy of racial integration and pledged to develop a continuous program to achieve the goal of integration of the Chicago Public Schools. "Although this resolution was in keeping with the board's agreement in the Webb case, no changes in the racial patterning of the school system or the deployment of resources emerged."[80] The promise of the Board of Education was a hollow one because no changes were made as to where students could attend school, nor was the equal use of resources included.

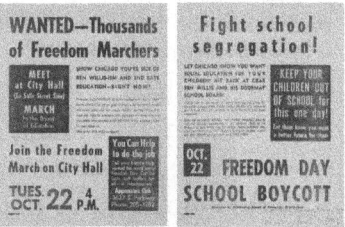

Freedom Day Boycott Chicago Poster, 1963.

---

80 Anderson and Pickering, *Confronting the Color Line*, 118.

Superintendent Willis and the School Board were having serious disagreements among themselves over the issue of transferring students to schools outside their neighborhoods. By the middle of October, the Board and Willis had reconciled their two positions. The activists for integration continued to demand that Willis be removed and that the schools be integrated. The CCCO organized a boycott of the schools and a demonstration at the Board of Education offices. The CCCO issued an official statement to the press declaring that on Tuesday, October 22, 1963, a Freedom Day Boycott would be held. The CCCO identified the motive for the boycott as protesting the inferior education given to all children in Chicago, the growing segregation in Chicago, the disgraceful behavior of Willis in ignoring the directives of the Board of Education, and the failure of the Board to fulfill its constituted authority. Along with this statement, the CCCO submitted a list of thirteen demands to the Board of Education.

On the day of the boycott, under the banner of Freedom Day, over two hundred thousand pupils from segregated schools stayed out of school. Over ten thousand people, black and white, marched to the offices of the Board of Education demanding the removal of Willis and the integration of the schools. That same day the school board released the results of the racial headcount which they had committed to do after the *Webb v. Board of Education* settlement.

> It showed a total enrollment of 536,163, of which 50.9 percent were white, 46.5 percent were black and 2.6 percent were "other." It further showed that 50.9 percent of the elementary pupils and 33.8 percent of the high school students were black and that 88 percent of the black elementary and 64 percent of the black high school students attended schools that were segregated (at least 90 percent black).[81]

Knowing that keeping the children out of school was harmful to them, Hattie and other activists from organizations such as the CCCO set up Freedom Schools in churches and community centers for the children to attend during the boycotts. The organization Teachers for Integrated Schools prepared and distributed teaching kits to Freedom School sites. Volunteers, including ministers, parents, and older students, taught elementary youth freedom songs and black history using the stories of

---

81 Anderson and Pickering, *Confronting the Color Line*, 120.

such people as Crispus Attucks, George Washington Carver, and Harriet Tubman. Students in Chicago Public Schools were not being taught anything about black history at any point in their school careers. Hattie was involved in setting up the Freedom Schools.

> We established what we called freedom schools. We had freedom schools where we even had just volunteers just working with the kids and we said down with Willis! And so we got rid of Willis, but we have a lot to learn. But just imagine. Now I've learned that you had a lot to learn—I was enthused, I was honest and I was sincere. But in ridding the schools of a superintendent, I see, I must confess, things are in a sorrier state today than they were in the 60s.

> I could tell you why I say that there is a regression. I do not see where integration of the school system will ever take place, but I see where our better teachers in the low-income black communities are sort of siphoned off and put in to integrate white schools. So the cream is siphoned off, so then we're left with full time basis. Substitute teachers and people have been completely demoralized by the system. And if that happens to a person, you can't do an effective job. You got to believe in what you're doing—got to have something there. And that spark is missing in many cases, so getting back to the civil rights movement. We boycotted the schools, we won some concessions, we did get the board to agree, they got rid of Benjamin Willis, but that also they agreed to high schools—Kenwood Academy and Martin Luther King high school, among other things throughout the city.[82]

Positive results of Freedom Day were that the CCCO realized that they had grassroots support from the black community, which gave them a mandate to continue working for change. Not only did the boycott demonstrate the support of the people, the release that same day of the racial statistics proved that segregation in the Chicago public schools was a fact.

After Freedom Day, Board President Roddewig and a twenty-person team from the CCCO met, but the meetings ended in frustration. For

---

82 Myers, interview, 23.

the mayor, the Board of Education, and the newspapers it was back to business as usual with meetings and hearings but no progress. Still maintaining that overcrowding, not segregation, was the problem, Willis and the Board of Education moved ahead with their plan to place mobile classrooms on black school campuses.

Following the success of the first Freedom Boycott, the leaders of CCCO called for a Freedom Day II boycott to be staged on February 25, 1964. At this point, there was dissension among the member organizations of CCCO. Some favored another boycott because they believed the first had made a difference, but others opposed it because they said it was illegal to keep children out of school. Unexpressed motives for opposition may have been that some of the organizations within CCCO received funding from some of the powerful people and organizations that opposed the boycott. Despite mounting opposition from politicians, the civil rights leaders, clergy, and other groups supported CCCO as it continued to organize and defend the boycott efforts. On Freedom Day II, 17,350 students stayed home from school. Estimates of the number of people who attended the demonstration at the Board of Education varied from 650 to 4,000 people.[83]

The Hauser panel, which had begun its research in September 1963, presented their report in March 1964.[84] It reported that 84 percent of black students attended black schools and 86 percent of white students were in white schools. The panel concluded that the segregation of black students was not intentional (de jure, by law) but was a result of the fact (de facto, socioeconomic conditions) that people lived in segregated neighborhoods. The panel acknowledged that in the Chicago Public School system black children were discriminated against solely based on skin color.

The panel made thirteen recommendations for public school improvement. The first four dealt with integration: that student reenrollment patterns be made more open for all students; that optimal use be made of all existing school facilities; that fostering racial integration be a major consideration for new schools and when drawing attendance

---

83 Anderson and Pickering, *Confronting the Color Line*, 41.
84 Advisory Panel on Integration of the Public Schools, *Integration of the Public Schools, Chicago*. See also the information in Anderson and Pickering, *Confronting the Color Line*, 134.

or district boundaries; that the Board of Education take positive steps to integrate faculties in the schools and teachers' colleges.

The next three recommendations were concerned with teachers: assure for all schools, as far as was legal and practicable, a fair distribution of teachers with varying lengths of experience and various types of professional credentials; vigorously encourage all teacher education centers in the Chicago area to develop more effective programs for the education of teachers for schools with high student turnover, heavy retardation, and limited education achievement; that in-service training include the history of minority groups in America and the world at large, the content and method of teaching children of different cultural heritages and human relations practices.

The final six recommendations were to substantially increase budget funds for acquisition of learning resources; identify the educational programs in elementary schools; increase counseling services in high schools and elementary schools; undertake a pilot program that would utilize as much best educational practice as possible; work to obtain funds that the panel's recommendations required; and, pursue effective communication between school and community and within the public school system.

When Hattie spoke to congregations and groups throughout the Chicago area, she often mentioned the caliber of teachers in black schools. Her view was that white teachers were assigned to black schools when they failed in white schools. She would also point out that teachers in black schools had less experience than those in white schools—an average of four years for black teachers and twelve for white teachers. At the same time, she never hesitated to call attention to teachers of quality who taught valiantly under the worst of conditions.

Under the existing conditions, a white principal did not have to state a reason for not hiring a black teacher. If the principal believed that black teachers were poor teachers or if the principal simply disliked black people, the black applicant teacher would not be hired. Two fears also fueled the prejudice that prevented many good black teachers from being hired. One was that white parents would object to their children being taught by a black person, and the second was that having black teachers on a staff would lower the prestige of the school.

The Board responded to the report with seven resolutions. One reaffirmed the Board's commitment to desegregation. The Board referred to a special committee the recommendations on pupil open enrollment patterns, optimal use of space, and location of schools and boundaries.

After the success of the 1963 boycott, things were calmer while civil rights groups struggled to design a plan that would move them forward in the fight against school segregation. The movement came to life again in March 1965 when forty ministers, symbolizing the forty days of Lent, picketed City Hall with weekly demonstrations. For the culmination on Good Friday, 2,500 demonstrators showed up at City Hall to participate in what was titled "Good Friday Witness Against Willis."[85] Even though the turnout was disappointing, the effort reenergized the fight against Willis. Despite years of anti-Willis protests, the Board of Education renewed his contract. The Board met in May of that year and, after a heated discussion, decided to renew Willis's contract for a full four years with the condition that he would retire once he reached the age of 65, which he did in 1966.

On June 10, 1965, 120,000 students stayed out of school. The next day 252 marchers were arrested and charged with obstructing traffic and disorderly conduct. After several days of marches and arrests and a rally at Buckingham Fountain, Willis promised to retire at age 65, which he did.

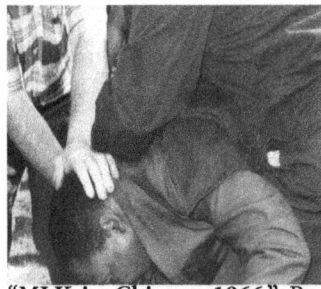

"MLK in Chicago 1966." Reprinted in: Past MLK Critics Face Twitter Backlash after Celebrating his Legacy Today, January 21, 2019. Photo credit: Larry Nocerino. Used by permission: *Chicago Sun-Times*.

In 1966 Martin Luther King Jr. chose Chicago as the site for his Northern campaign against racism. The Chicago Freedom Movement, as the campaign was called, focused originally on slum housing. Having observed the fight for integrated public education in Chicago, King and his colleagues believed that the black community in Chicago was strong enough and united enough to help advance the fight against racism that King and others were waging in the South.

King moved his family into an apartment in the Woodlawn area of Chicago to show his commitment to open housing. Woodlawn

---

85 See Anderson and Pickering, *Confronting the Color Line*, 152-53.

was another black ghetto similar in many ways to Bronzeville, though not as large. To protest housing segregation, King and his aides went to Marquette Park, a white enclave on Chicago's southwest side. They and the seven hundred people who were marching with them were attacked with a rain of rocks, bottles, and firecrackers. A placard carried by a white protester read, "King would look good with a knife in his back." King was struck by a rock and fell to his knees. Thirty people were injured, and forty arrests were made. King later explained why he put himself at risk: "I have to do this—to expose myself—to bring this hate into the open." He had done that before, but Chicago was different. "I have seen many demonstrations in the South, but I have never seen anything so hostile and so hateful as I've seen here today," he said.[86]

King and Chicago civil rights advocates met with Mayor Richard J. Daley. However, even King came up against an immovable wall when he met with Daley. Their conference was unproductive, and King's peaceful marches were met with violence. King said that they didn't get a cold reception but neither did they get any commitments.

Describing her contact with King, Hattie said,

> …this thing that happened during the civil rights movement was like a charisma that just hit the whole race of people where ever you were. I would say a once-in-a-lifetime in our lifetime would we see a man of that stature, whatever you want to call it. I just don't think there's anybody who would fill his shoes right through here… I can't say that I knew Dr. King or walked with him. I met him at the time that he came to Chicago when he marched in Cicero. He had an apartment on the West side. I forget the address. But it was very difficult to walk over there and just get to see Dr. Martin Luther King Jr. He was closely guarded and you didn't get in. And so in order for our group of PTA and the people in this area—the grassroots—we had to go through Andrew Young—he was with Dr. King in those days—and he wasn't even living in Chicago, but we had to send our request in that way to get through, even though King was in

---

[86] Frank James, "Martin Luther King Jr. in Chicago," *Chicago Tribune*, January 3, 2008, unpaged, https://www.chicagotribune.com/news/nationworld/politics/chi-chicagodays-martinlutherking-story-story.html.

> Chicago, because of the circumstances. He had to be closely guarded.[87]

In this interview, she went on to talk about the how Mayor Daley and some of the black ministers did not want King in Chicago. Hattie quoted them as saying that King didn't belong in Chicago, he belonged in the South because he didn't know anything about the North.

> That was the surprising horror of the civil rights movement, was to see politicians that were black like our alderman, Claude Holman, he would get on TV here anywhere and say, "wild horses wouldn't take me from the side of the mayor." Mayor Daley was alive then, and his lackey was an alderman of this ward. So what I'm saying is Daley didn't want him in Chicago, and many of the black ministers who were straight Democrat people—they were part of the Democrat machine—for the rewards, for the concessions, for the patronage jobs, they would go to their parishioners in the church.[88]

Hattie met strong opposition in Olivet Baptist Church where her father was an active member. She was helping publicize the rally that King planned to hold at Soldier Field on July 10, 1966, as part of the Chicago Freedom Movement. As she was handing out flyers, the pastor's wife came and pulled the flyers out of the hands of the people and from Hattie.

> People were just standing there aghast, and she's taking back these little one-page flyers about Dr. King. So these are the kinds of situations that I'm talking about at grassroots level that went on during that time. But many people really rallied behind Dr. King in prayer. They didn't know anything else to do. Many of us who could do a little more, we did. I think that it still stands to this day that many of us realize what the coming of Dr. Martin Luther King Jr. meant to the human race. There's other people who are benefiting from everything he stood for.[89]

---

87 Myers, interview, 26.
88 Myers, interview, 28.
89 Myers, interview, 29.

When Willis retired in 1966, James Francis Redmond succeeded him as superintendent and served until 1975. Redmond attempted to develop integration plans that would send black students to predominantly white schools by means of racial quotas instead of set boundaries. He wanted to bus students to schools outside their neighborhoods.

White parents and various groups accused Redmond of advocating for social change instead of educational ones when he spoke for busing students. In the midst of these accusations, he was interviewed by a reporter from the *Chicago Tribune*. He said, "In our kind of society today, there is good in knowing and working with people of other races. This is part of the educational experience that citizens of an emerging society must have. I don't believe that those who think they are threatened by this have understood the purpose."[90] In 1975, Redmond announced that he would not seek another term as general superintendent.

On July 24, 1975, Joseph P. Hannon was appointed to be the superintendent for a four-year term. Along with the inherited problems from previous superintendents' administrations, Hannon faced the specter that the federal Department of Health, Education, and Welfare (HEW) threatened to take away $100 million in federal funding because the school district failed to integrate the faculties of its schools.

HEW announced that it would continue negotiations with the Board if it would agree to HEW's definition of a desegregated school. The federal standard to determine whether a school was desegregated was when the student body was 25 to 50 percent white and 50 to 75 percent black. The Chicago Board of Education's determination as to whether a school was desegregated fell far short of the federal standard. In the policy of the Board, a school was desegregated when it had no more than 90 percent of its students belonging to only one race. In other words, if 90 percent of the student population in a school was black, the school was considered to be desegregated. Likewise, if the school was composed of 90 percent white students, the Board considered it desegregated.

Superintendent Hannon submitted a plan called *Access to Excellence* to HEW, which acknowledged that although there were many sound educational programs in the plan it did not correct the unlawful segregated

---

90 "James Redmond Looks Back Over His First Year on the Job," *Chicago Tribune*, October 1, 1967.

conditions that had been identified. Hannon held firmly to his conviction that integration should be voluntary and that busing students to schools out of their neighborhood in order to achieve desegregation was unacceptable.

On August 31, 1975, the federal officials at HEW developed a proposal for the Chicago public schools that required the mandatory busing of 114,000 elementary students. The Board was not required to accept the proposal, but if it chose to do so the result would be the desegregation of 60 percent of the district's schools and would involve 55 percent of the district student population. The Board responded that busing children to schools outside their neighborhood to achieve the government's definition of integration would be costly and would not improve education.

Hannon vehemently denied the charges against his school district but agreed to cooperate with HEW to resolve the desegregation issue in hopes of reclaiming federal funding. Later that year the Board applied to HEW requesting funds for the 1980-1981 school year, but the request was denied again. By this time a coalition of black civic and church leaders was urging the Board to remove Hannon. He resigned on January 25, 1980. His resignation came when the Board, seeking loans to pay off loans, lost its credit rating.

In April 1980, Dr. Ruth Love was appointed to succeed Hannon as superintendent. She was the first black person to hold that office. As Love took office, the state ordered that a Chicago School Finance Authority be appointed to oversee the system's budget. At the same time, the United States Department of Justice announced that it was going to sue the Chicago Public Schools Board of Education, alleging that the Board engaged in acts of discrimination in the assignment to particular schools of both students and teachers in violation of federal law.

Instead of taking the matter to court, the two parties reached a legal agreement called a "consent decree," an order issued by a judge based upon an agreement between two parties to a lawsuit instead of going to trial. The consent decree alleged that the Board of Education operated a dual school system that segregated students on the basis of race and ethnic origin in violation of the equal protection clause of the 19th Amendment to the United States Constitution and Title IV and Title VI of the Civil Rights Act of 1964. The court would have full jurisdiction over the consent decree and would be the one to determine when it could be terminated.

The consent decree required the Chicago Public Schools to implement a voluntary desegregation plan to create and maintain as many racially integrated schools as possible. In response, the Board set up a Committee on Desegregation to meet with the United States Department of Justice to try to resolve the district's legal issues.

The Committee reached an agreement with the Department of Justice that centered on a three-step process to eradicate segregation in the schools. First, the Board would determine principles that would guide the development of a plan. Second, the Board would adopt a detailed plan no later than March 1981. Third, the plan would be implemented in September 1981.

The Committee on Desegregation recommended that the Board accept the terms of the proposed consent decree and seek to have it judicially approved. It was approved, providing that the Chicago Public Schools Board of Education would work out a viable plan to solve the problem of student desegregation and that it would correct areas that hindered the schools' eligibility for federal funding such as classroom integration, bilingual program staffing, and faculty assignment. The plan would be developed over a period of time from October 15 to March 31, 1981, when the plan would be conveyed to the Department of Justice and filed with the Court. After working on the plan for two years the Board sent it to Judge Milton Shadur, of the United States District Court for the Northern District of Illinois. Another year passed before the judge approved it.

The Board's stand was ambiguous, neither acknowledging nor denying allegations set before them. The Board acknowledged that the segregation of students hindered their education. While it agreed that the school system suffered from racially isolated schools, it also submitted that it would be financially difficult to address the issues.

In 1986 Hattie said:

> As I look back on it now, I haven't seen too much change. I've seen things even worsen since then. As much as I thought a superintendent of schools could change, I found that they

are at the top of the whole mess, but they can't change all of the whole system. And at that time there were many changes, I forget just what all they were, because I was zeroing in on the achievement, the lack of educational opportunities. Misappropriation of monies and funds—I don't know just what all they accused Dr. Willis of at the time. In fact, I've seen things worse. And so, under other superintendents, until I found that really wasn't the solution. If I had it to do over again, I don't think that I would have the same attitude that I had.

I feel that the Board of Education, the system as it existed then and as it exists now, is the persons that cover up dirt, sweep it under the rug—they're the ones that get promoted upstairs, in other words, they get the bigger job. They are district superintendents, and they are the ones that get the promotions.... So I can't see a black superintendent of schools as being instrumental in bringing about quality education in the system.[91]

The segregation of students in the public schools in Chicago was a well-known fact attested to by then Secretary of Education William Bennett. At a forum on education on November 7, 1987, Bennett called the Chicago Public Schools the worst in the nation and added that it would take a "man or woman of steel" to clean up Chicago's school system, the third largest in the nation after New York and Los Angeles.[92]

The period between the approval of the plan and 1995 lacked parent demonstrations and boycotts like the ones in the 1960s, but the Chicago Teachers' Union and other groups kept alive the demands for integration. Hattie's struggle with recurring brain tumors prohibited her continued participation in the fight for equal education for black students but her passion for equality for black youth never waned.

In 1995 the state legislature passed the Chicago School Reform Amendatory Act, which granted complete control of the schools to Mayor Richard M. Daley. This action concentrated power over school policies

---

91 Myers, interview, 42.
92 "Schools in Chicago Are Called the Worst by Education Chief," *New York Times*, November 8, 1987, unpaged, https://www.nytimes.com/1987/11/08/us/schools-in-chicago-are-called-the-worst-by-education-chief.html.

in the hands of the mayor and the Chicago Public Schools Central Office and gave the mayor sole authority over the schools. From then on it was the mayor's job to appoint Board of Education members and to select the board president. It took power from the hands of local school councils, which had been created by the Chicago School Reform Act in 1988 and made major decision-making regarding education less democratic. Decisions were increasingly directed by the business community and politicians with less input from educators.[93]

A business model replaced the old organization. Instead of a superintendent of schools, a Chief Executive Officer and an Office of Accountability were implemented, the theory being that the business model would lead to immediate and substantial improvement. The opposite of that model was that educators work under a method that involves research and a pilot plan that may take years to implement.

The Chicago Board of Education operated under a consent decree (1980), a modified consent decree (2001), and a second Modified Consent Agreement (2006). Each consent decree had the objective of desegregating the Chicago Public Schools. The goals and objectives set forth in all three versions of the consent decree were in keeping with the objectives of *Brown v. Board*. However, over the span of twenty-five years, there had been significant demographic changes in Chicago's neighborhoods and schools.

In 2001, the United States and the Chicago Public Schools reviewed the school district's implementation of and compliance with the original consent decree. It was determined that almost all areas were covered but that full compliance had not been reached. As a result, the United States and the Board of Education entered into a Modified Consent Decree. It was designed with the intention that its full implementation would address the goals that were set forth in the original consent decree and established a timetable that would bring the case to a final resolution. It alluded to the reality that Chicago's distinctive separation of neighborhoods was also reflected in the organization of students within their neighborhood schools. Both parties recognized that the size and demographics of the school system made it impossible for all schools to be

---

93 Carol Caref et al., *The Black and White of Education in Chicago Public Schools, Class, Charters and Chaos* (Chicago: Chicago Teachers Union, 2012), 8, www.teachersolidarity.com/.../the-black-and-white-of-education-in-chicago-s-public-schools.

desegregated. The parties agreed that the Board of Education would use a variety of strategies, including magnet and charter schools, and would establish and maintain as many schools as possible with desegregated enrollments. Requirements were also established regarding balance in the racial and ethnic composition of faculty.

In 2005, the courts asked both parties if provisions of the Modified Consent Decree should continue. A formal hearing was scheduled for May 15, 2006, to address the question. Because of the significant changes in the racial demographics of Chicago's neighborhoods the student population of the Chicago Public Schools in 2005 was entirely different from that which existed in 1980 at the time of the original consent decree. As a result of the court's inquiry and further discovery by both parties, the United States and the Board of Education of the City of Chicago jointly requested that they vacate the Modified Consent Decree and be allowed to enter a Second Amended Consent Decree. The court approved the request to enter a Second Amended Consent Decree but established that it could not automatically expire unless the court made the decision that it should expire.[94]

The change in demographics can be explained partially by "white flight" from the city to suburban communities. However, it also reflected a shift to private and parochial school education for many white children. By the 1990s, two-thirds of Chicago's white students attended private schools. The city's school-age population had become substantially divided between two types of schools, a majority black public system (with growing numbers of Hispanics) and a mainly white system of parochial and other private schools.

On September 24, 2009, the Supreme Court of the United States determined that the Chicago Public Schools had achieved unitary status. This essentially meant that in the opinion of the Court the district demonstrated substantial good faith compliance with the desegregation mandates of the Second Modified Consent Decree to the extent practical. Thus, in the judgment of the Court, remnants of past discrimination had been eliminated and judicial oversight was no longer warranted. This ruling returned control of all admissions processes to the Chicago Public

---

94 Shawn L. Jackson, "An Historical Analysis of the Chicago Public Schools Desegregation Consent Decree (1980-2006)," (PhD diss., Loyola University, 2010), 129, http://ecommons.luc.edu/luc_diss/129.

Schools and mandated that the schools could not continue to use race as a criterion for admission of any student to any school.

Key words in the court's determination are "...to the extent practical." The word "practical" allows an escape hatch for those who don't see the need for or care about equal education for children of all races. In the situation of the Chicago Public Schools in 2009, it was argued that it was not practical to remove students from their segregated neighborhoods to integrate any white schools. Doing so would be cumbersome and would require students to travel long distances to an integrated school. It was also argued that it was not practical because there truly was a budget crisis and the school district could not afford to move students around.

In 2013, Mayor Rahm Emanuel and the Board of Education announced that forty-nine public schools would be closed, most of them on the South Side and the West Side of Chicago, where the population majority is black. As might have been expected, the mayor and the school board maintained that their actions were not racist. A writer for the *Chicago Tribune* described the mayor's vision in these words: "...for a downsized school system, which he argues will help combat massive budget deficit and allow the district to distribute scarce resources more efficiently."[95]

In addition to the negative effect of school closings on black students, a strong argument can be made that closing a school is akin to closing a community. Public schools, both urban and rural, are often the glue that holds a community together.

The trend that Mayor Emanuel and the School Board are pursuing, indeed fostering, is the trend toward charter schools in place of public schools. The establishment of charter schools and the promotion of them are indebted to the contributions of millionaires and their foundations.

What Hattie and countless other people worked so hard and so passionately for has still not been achieved either in Chicago or in our nation as a whole. Article 3 of the Northwest Ordinance declared: "Religion, morality, and knowledge being necessary to good government and the

---

[95] Noreen S. Ahmed-Ullah, John Chase, and Bob Sector, "CPS Approves Largest School Closing in Chicago History," *Chicago Tribune*, May 23, 2013, https://www.google.com/url?sa=t&rct=j&q=&esrc=s&source=web&cd=1&cad=rja&uact=8&ved=2ahUKEwj4v5CN1_fAhUPvKwKHcPnAKoQFjAAegQICRAB&url=https%3A%2F%2Fwww.chicagotribune.com%2Fnews%2Fct-xpm-2013-05-23-chi-chicago-school-closings-20130522-story.html&usg=AOvVaw2agOQR43u-PBz-sUOoNn6H.

happiness of mankind, schools and the means of education shall forever be encouraged." The vision of the Northwest Territory awaits fulfillment after more than two hundred years.

Chapter 9
POLITICS

In 1973, the death of Alderman Claude W. B. Holman set the stage for Hattie to run for the office of alderman in a special election. Holman had been the alderman for the 4th Ward for over two decades and was a staunch supporter of Mayor Richard J. Daley. Just days before his death, Holman had proudly proclaimed, "I am a puppet for Mayor Daley."[96]

Holman was one of six black aldermen on the City Council who were dubbed the "Silent Six." These six, from predominantly black wards, were not allowed to speak or participate in Council proceedings unless they received a signal from Daley's floor leader or from Daley himself. Two white aldermen, Leon Depres and David Llorens, are credited with being "more negro" than these six because they were more oriented to civil rights than were the black members.

Hattie's preferred means of action was through churches, colleges, seminaries, nonprofit organizations, and individuals, but at every turn in her work in the community she encountered the politics that drove the city of Chicago. By serving the people as an alderman, Hattie would be continuing to fulfill the vow she made after her brain surgery in 1966: to serve God by helping people. The dilapidated public housing where so many of her friends and neighbors lived existed because of politics. The joblessness that kept families poor and hungry existed because of politics. The poor quality of education for the children of Oakland existed because of politics. The poor policing of the area existed because of politics.

Wards are legislative districts that are the foundation of the government of the city of Chicago. The city is divided into fifty wards, each represented on the City Council by an alderman who is elected by the voters in the ward. Each ward is divided into fifty-two election precincts headed by a precinct captain. Hattie had served in that role in her precinct. The main

---

[96] Doug Cassell, "Is Tim Evans for Real? *Chicago Reader*, March 16, 1989, http://m.chicagoreader.com/chicago/is-tim-evans-for-real/Content?oid=873531.

job of a precinct captain is to get votes for the candidate of their party by communicating with the people in the precinct. The precinct captain is the main communications tool for the alderman.

The Fourth Ward Independent Political Coalition presented Hattie as a candidate who would run a good race and be progressive in working on the problems of the ward if she was elected.

> So at one time, I would say it was about 13 years ago, the people here—all those fold up chairs you see (14+) were all filled up here, at meetings we have here sometimes on Saturday afternoons. So they say, "Why don't you run for alderman?" Well, fools rush in where angels fear to tread. And I allowed the people to run all around and get petitions and in three weeks' time my hat was in the ring for alderman of this Ward. So I learned a lot from it and I don't regret it, and I gave the alderman—the regular machine candidate, a really hard time. But I learned from it that I would never be active politically again. I thought I was doing a good thing because I was asked.[97]

The coalition set up a headquarters at 1126 East 47th Street and proceeded to organize a campaign. According to minutes of their meeting on October 10, 1973, a Social Committee was appointed to organize campaign-sponsored events such as open houses and rallies, large public gatherings, and home gatherings at which Hattie would be present.

The coalition planned that beginning on October 13 the candidate would be scheduled for two meetings per evening during the week. During the last two weeks of the campaign, Hattie would make appearances in the afternoons. In addition, the schedule planned three to four events on weekend days. Hattie was present at this meeting so she must have agreed to such a rigorous schedule. Members of the committee were responsible for these events and for coffees to be held in the homes of supporters.

As the campaign progressed, Hattie was outspoken and direct in her plans for serving as the alderman of the 4th Ward. She described the ward as the place where the most impoverished people in Chicago lived,

---
97 Myers, interview, 9.

saying, "When I'm elected alderman in this ward I know what I'll do first. I'll have it declared a disaster area." In her campaign speeches and interviews, Hattie called attention to the fact that in the neighborhood there were ten fires a month in buildings that housed poor families. These places were not rebuilt or cleared, so the area looked like a bombed city from World War II. The physical condition of the buildings and lots contributed to the high rates of tuberculosis, infant mortality, and crime.

Hattie's motivation for seeking the office of alderman was expressed in an interview published in the *Chicago Tribune* on November 24, 1973. "I just got tired of seeing how insignificant black life is to many agencies. An awareness of how insensitive the plantation rule is to our needs is one reason I am in this." She concluded this interview with these words: "I've always been accused of starting something, and now I am."[98]

A time-honored practice that angered Hattie greatly was patronage—aldermen gave whatever jobs became available to people who were loyal to the Democratic Party, more specifically to Mayor Daley. She felt that the use of patronage was a way to keep black people not only begging and kowtowing for the sake of jobs but intimidated in how they voted. The intimidation included threats of paychecks for work they did being held up or their rents being increased.

Chicago has long served as an example of the deep-seated corruption of elected officials. The University of Illinois at Chicago and the University of Illinois' Institute of Government and Public Affairs released a study in December 2012 naming Chicago the most corrupt city in the nation. The report, "Chicago and Illinois: Leading the Pack in Corruption,"[99] cites federal data showing that in the years between 1976 and 2010 there were 1,531 convictions for public corruption in the federal district dominated by Chicago. That there is corruption at the state level is attested to by the fact that since the 1970s, four of Illinois' seven governors have spent time or are spending time in prison.

---

98 Yla Eason, "Hattie's Shaking the Ties That Bind," Tempo, *Chicago Tribune*, December 12, 1973, 18.
99 Dick Simpson, James Nowlan, Thomas J. Gradel & Melissa Mouritsen Zmuda et al., *Chicago and Illinois, Leading the Pack in Corruption*, Chicago, University of Illinois at Chicago, February 15, 2012, 1-17, http://docplayer.net/55534460-Chicago-and-illinois-leading-the-pack-in-corruption.html.

Following the pattern of corruption, the city of Chicago has seen its share of convicted officials. The first conviction of Chicago aldermen and Cook County Commissioners for accepting bribes to rig a contract occurred in 1869. Since 1973, thirty-one aldermen have been convicted of corruption. Approximately one hundred aldermen have served prison time since then, a conviction rate of about one-third. The corruption at high levels of government is accompanied by all kinds of graft and deceit at lower levels as well. This environment of corruption stymied many of Hattie's hopes and dreams for all people, but especially for the people in her neighborhood.

One of the planks in her election campaign was to eliminate the patronage system in the 4th Ward. An article about her campaign in the *Chicago Tribune* quoted her as saying: "The jobs are a tool to keep us on our knees." She stated that one thousand people who have patronage jobs are so desperate they will vote with the machine, which keeps all black people down.[100]

Hattie never talked to me about politics as such, but she did say that whenever a new business would open in her neighborhood the alderman would decide who got the jobs. It is the patronage for which Chicago is famous. Seeing that kind of thing happening over her lifetime was certainly one of the contributing factors that convinced Hattie to run for the office of alderman.

She was also personally aware of the poor quality of public schools that black children attended. The study center she started in a storefront where children would have a safe, affirming place to study was burned down by an arsonist. Hattie and others suspected that it was done under the direction of Alderman Holman, whose position she would be filling if she won the election. She saw the destruction of her school as one of the ways ward politics had of bringing black folks to their knees.

Politics in themselves are not a bad thing and are at work in every aspect of human life. Politics are the way people relate to each other in terms of ideas, power, and authority. There are politics within schools, workplaces, churches, and families as well as in government. In the best of situations, people have at heart an overall goal of the well-being of all who are involved in the entity. But in places where the stakes are

---

100 Eason, "Hattie's Shaking the Ties," 17.

high in terms of power and wealth, the well-being of all can easily slip away, and self-seeking behavior readily barges in. The dishonesty and greed that often accompany personal ambition corrupt politicians and the institutions where they hold sway. Corrupt politics were and are practiced with concern only for one's own advancement, power, and accumulation of wealth.

Hattie was an astute observer of the way politics in Chicago operated almost always to the detriment of black people. Her running for the office of alderman was a combination of her own passion for justice and the confidence that many of the people in the 4th Ward had in her. Whatever the pressures, whether from herself or others, her motivation was to be in a position from which she could affect the well-being not only of the people in Kenwood/Oakland but throughout Chicago.

Hattie's opponent in the election was Democrat Timothy C. Evans, an attorney and acting 4th Ward Democratic Committeeman who had graduated from John Marshall Law School in 1969. Being interested in city politics, he joined the city of Chicago's Department of Investigations and became a deputy commissioner. His mentor in Democratic politics was Claude W. B. Holman, for whose seat Hattie and Evans were running. Even though he was young and new to Chicago, Evans was firmly a part of the Democratic machine that ran Chicago.

The Chicago newspapers described the two candidates by playing on the contrast between the two. Evans's list of credentials was always highlighted: 4th Ward Democratic Committeeman (succeeding Holman), graduate of the University of Illinois and John Marshall Law School, treasurer of the Cook County Bar Association, Chief Officer for the Cook County Securities Division of the Secretary of State's Office.

This description of Evans was usually followed by this description of Hattie, who was running as an Independent: fifty years old, mother of six children, Girl Scout Executive, 4th Ward civil rights activist for thirty years. One paper, the *Chicago Defender*, did state that Hattie "has the insight on the need for joint action by the alderman and community groups, PTA councils, business organizations in the community to prevent and resolve problems."[101]

---

[101] Ted Watson, "Contests in 4th, 7th Ward Battles Heat Up," *Chicago Defender*, October 15, 1973, 11.

During the campaign, Mayor Daley visited the 4th Ward in support of Evans. The announced purpose of the mayor's visit was to attend a groundbreaking of the Martin Luther King Jr. Community Service Center and a ceremony renaming a local health center as Claude Holman Health Center. It may be that only someone who lives or has lived in Chicago can realize the power and influence of that mayor, popularly called "Hizzoner." Daley served as mayor for six four-year terms. He dominated the city's politics and government with little tolerance for dissent, and his Board of Education kept the schools racially segregated. Claims were made in a newspaper article that black regular Democratic organization precinct members and patronage jobholders from other black wards came in droves to support Evans.[102] The writer accused them of using the tactics of harassment, coercion, and intimidation to achieve their goal of electing Evans.

Individuals who supported Hattie included the influential black leaders Al Raby and Timuel Black. Al Raby was a co-leader with Martin Luther King Jr. in the civil rights movement. The *Chicago Metro News* on November 27, 1971, quoted Raby as saying that he and Martin Luther King Jr. were hailed as the leaders of the civil rights movement in Chicago in the 1960s because they were in the limelight. But, he said, the real leaders were people like Hattie Williams.[103]

Timuel Black, who also was prominent in the civil rights movement in Chicago, was one of the leaders of the Coordinating Council of Community Organizations when the CCCO staged a series of boycotts in 1963 to demand desegregation in overcrowded public schools. He was heavily involved in Martin Luther King Jr.'s Chicago Freedom Movement and was part of an interracial group of students at the University of Chicago who established the Congress of Racial Equality in 1942.

Besides being supported by these influential men, Hattie was endorsed by several organizations, the League of Black Women. She was also endorsed by the aldermen of four other wards. The Rev. Jesse Jackson, founder of Operation PUSH (People United to Save Humanity), was an important supporter.

---

102 Phil Smith, "Why White Folks Are Still in the Lead?" *Chicago Metro News*, December 8, 1973, 3.
103 "Al Raby Supports Hattie Williams—In the 4th Ward," *Chicago Metro News*, November 24, 1973, 2.

The *Chicago Tribune* endorsed Hattie's candidacy on November 25, 1973, stating that she would provide responsive leadership and give the people of the 4th Ward a voice in and power over their local government that they had not previously had.[104] The endorsement said that the 4th Ward needed a leader, not another follower of the machine. The *Chicago Sun-Times* endorsed her on November 21, 1973, saying that her campaign was outspoken on reform of public housing, public education, welfare, and other programs.[105]

The problems faced in the Oakland area (the 4th Ward) were the very problems that Hattie worked to counteract: absentee landlords, black urban removal, white real estate interests taking over the vacant land in order to return it to white occupancy, overcrowded schools, poor public protection, unclean streets, poor garbage removal, building violations, and gang activity. As she campaigned, Hattie said, "One of my biggest projects is to seek a way to decrease crime in the area and to make the community residents aware of methods to be used in contacts for that purpose." Hattie told me, a white woman, that I was safe coming to her home in this crime-ridden area. In her experience, I was safer there than she was. "The police are all white. If someone hurts you, they will round up every black man within thirteen blocks looking for the guilty man. If someone hurts me, a black woman, the white police won't do anything. They don't care."

Hattie's concerns and work covered all the systemic ills that her neighbors lived under as well as issues that faced the whole city. An example of Hattie's courage and outspokenness is apparent in one of the campaign speeches she gave. She was speaking to the congregation of the First Unitarian Church of Chicago on the issue of collective municipal employees in Chicago.

> The attitude of the Daley administration toward the unions with which it deals typifies its attitude toward the people in general: stay in your place, don't ask questions, and you will be taken care of. This relationship is as destructive of human dignity and self-respect in the particular application as it is in the general.[106]

---

104 "Our Aldermanic Choices," *Chicago Tribune,* November 25, 1973, A4.
105 "For Mrs. Williams in 4th Ward," *Chicago Sun-Times,* November 21, 1978, 25.
106 "4th Ward Candidate Blasts Daley Machine," *Chicago Metro News,* November 10, 1973, 1.

In the election for alderman, Timothy Evans received 6,784 votes and Hattie received 3,136. Only 38 percent of the eligible voters in the 4th Ward exercised their right to vote. On December 8, 1973, a columnist for the *Chicago Metro News* described the race for the 4th Ward alderman as "another case of the Christians being thrown into the lions' den. And while the Christians had a whole lot of heart, the lion still doomed them."[107]

After his election, Evans became a strong supporter of Hattie's efforts to right the wrongs in the 4th Ward. Hattie's son Bernard wrote that his mother and Evans worked together, and that Evans was always invited to and attended special events that Hattie organized such as back-to-school and book club events. As alderman, Evans worked in a positive way on several problems that directly impacted the people in Kenwood Oakland.

In one of the first conversations we had with Hattie, she told us that the city would one day soon demolish the Chicago Housing Authority's housing across the street from her house. The plan, as she saw it, was to move residents out under the promise of their having first chance on renovated apartments. When the people were out of their homes, Hattie predicted, the buildings would be torn down. New buildings would be built but there would not be enough units for all the people who previously lived there and the rents would be too high for the former residents to pay. That was serious enough, but equally troubling was the fact that the people had nowhere to go when they moved out of their homes in the high-rise public housing buildings.

By 1985, Hattie's prophecy was becoming reality. A developer proposed to demolish six Chicago Housing Authority high-rises across Lake Street from Hattie's home. Evans was opposed to the plan. In a *Chicago Tribune* article in 1988, as the plan was being debated, Evans was quoted as saying," I believe in community improvement, self-determination, development that minimizes displacement and a principle that says a government that makes a promise must keep that promise."[108] Hattie, Evans, and countless others knew that the housing authority would not keep the promises it made that displaced tenants would have the right to return as tenants in the Lake Front Properties.

---

107 Smith, "Why White Folk?," 3.
108 "Ald. Evans Rips Series in *Tribune*," *Chicago Tribune*, September 1, 1988, 1.

Hattie was defeated in electoral politics, but that only increased her zeal to be a change agent in the politics that operated between her neighbors and the governing powers including the Chicago Housing Authority and the Chicago Board of Education. She said, "I am not in politics, but if you live and breathe, you're in politics."[109]

---

109 Myers, interview, 9.

Chapter 10
HATTIE'S PRAYERS

Hattie told me this story of how she was moved to prayer and to give herself to her community. In 1966, when she was forty-four years old, she was diagnosed with a malignant tumor on her pituitary gland. As she faced surgery to remove it, she prayed to God to let her survive because her children needed her if they were to grow up to be good and decent people. At the time four of her boys were teenagers. She promised God that she would serve him through ministry and service in her neighborhood.

Hattie's surgery was successful, and she was sent home with a supply of hormone shots with which she would have to inject herself every day for the rest of her life in order to stay alive. When she was getting ready to give herself the first shot, she praised God for giving her life back. At that moment she decided she didn't need the shots, so she didn't take them.

> I remember the doctor saying at Michael Reese that I was going to have to take a certain drug for the rest of my life because of the removal of the pituitary gland, that I would have to take protessentannin [This was how it was spelled in the interview transcript. I haven't been able to find this word anywhere else.] a drug, to keep me from being dehydrated, and I would die if I didn't take this particular drug. I asked the Lord, "If you have given me my sight and the activity of my limbs and I am able to praise you, why do I have to take this? I took that needle—all my kids were in school—and I asked the Lord, why do I have to do this?" A deep peace came over me, and I walked in faith. I laid the needle down, and I haven't had another shot from that time to this day. So I thank God for that miracle. So all along the way there have been little affirmations and signs.[110]

---

110 Edwards, interview, 3.

When Hattie returned to Michael Reese Hospital a few weeks later for a post-surgery exam, the doctor told her he would write a new prescription for the shots. She said she didn't need it because she hadn't used any of the first batch he had given her. His response was that she couldn't live without it. She went home content that God had heard her prayer for recovery. She was even more determined to serve God in the people of her neighborhood.

The next day she received a phone call from the doctor's office telling her to check into Michael Reese Hospital right away. She was worried that another malignancy had been found or that something else was wrong, so she did as she was told. The next morning her surgeon and several other doctors came into her room with a group of student doctors all carrying clipboards. That really scared her, but her surgeon informed her that something had happened that never happens! He told her that her pituitary gland had grown back. If there had been any doubt in her mind, she knew for certain that God had much for her to do.

Whenever a group or an individual came into Hattie's home, she prayed with them. For her, every event, large or small, in her home or in someone else's, with a large group or with an individual, was an occasion for praying. Praying with Hattie was like holding onto a live current of electricity—you could feel the Holy Spirit pass through the hands of everyone in the circle.

Not only were her prayers that vibrant, it also seemed that whatever Hattie asked for she received. I am sure she prayed fervently for the well-being of people in her neighborhood and did not get exactly what she prayed for. Praying is not an exercise in asking a greater being to do you a favor. Prayer fosters a relationship with God that helps the one who prays learn how to pray. I am sure this is the kind of relationship Hattie had with God. That is why we saw so many instances of her requests being answered in just the way she expected. She asked for what was already in God's will because she was that close to God, that filled with the Spirit.

One of the activities that took place in Hattie's home was sewing classes. At one point one of the nuns who worked with Hattie was a quilter. She only had a short time to work with Hattie before she left for a mission in South America. Hattie wanted her to teach the women how to make quilts, so she prayed for quilt pieces. One day a neighbor of mine called me and asked if Hattie could use quilt pieces. I didn't know she was holding the quilting class, but I did know she had classes in which she taught women to make dresses for themselves and clothing for their children. I also knew that my neighbor had shelves full of dress lengths of material that she bought and didn't use. She was, in fact, a fabric hoarder. I said I would take quilt pieces, but that if she had any dress lengths Hattie could use them as well since she was having classes on dressmaking. This neighbor brought over four large black plastic garbage bags full of fabric. I didn't look into them so I don't know how much was scrap pieces and how much was yardage. When we took the bags into Hattie's living room, I apologized that they contained scraps of material. She said, "Praise God! I have been praying for pieces of fabric to make quilts!" There were just two weeks left before the nun left the country for her overseas assignment.

Another time a friend from church called and asked if Hattie could use the high- protein beverage Ensure. This friend's mother had been living on Ensure for several months preceding her death. A case of twenty-four cans of Ensure was available. I didn't think Hattie would have any use for it, but her words about letting her decide what she needed and what she didn't resounded in my mind. So Norm and I took the cans of Ensure to her along with our car's trunkful of food.

As Norm walked in the door carrying the box of Ensure, Hattie exclaimed, "Praise God! I was just praying for Ensure!" She was praying not for just any high-protein drink but for Ensure in particular. It was for a ninety-year-old woman who lived three doors away from Hattie. The woman had cancer, and her doctor had directed her to drink Ensure to get the nourishment she needed. She couldn't afford to buy as much as the doctor recommended so she was subsisting on one can a day. We walked with Hattie to this woman's home, which was a big old Victorian house like Hattie's, with Norm carrying the case of Ensure. We knocked on the door and could hear slow, shuffling footsteps coming down the hall. A tiny, shrunken woman the color of brown sugar opened the door and backed away so we could enter. When she saw what we were bringing to her, she raised her hands heavenward and shouted, "Praise Jesus!" Obviously twenty-four cans of this life-saving drink would not last forever, but maybe Hattie prayed for others to bring more.

The members of my husband's church, Christ Presbyterian Church, in the northwest suburb of Hanover Park, not only garbage picked and donated food, they also set up a fund to which they could donate money, kind of an emergency fund for Hattie. When she needed something that we couldn't salvage or solicit, we could draw on that fund to buy something or give it to her to give to someone who needed it. The sum of $241.63 had been in the bank untouched for several months.

The Comboni Fathers, an international Catholic missionary order, had a sixtieth birthday party in Hyde Park for Hattie to which we were invited. Norm decided that we needed to give her the balance of that account because it wasn't doing any good just sitting in the bank. Again, we didn't know she was praying for it, and she didn't know we had it. We walked into the living room of the home of the Comboni Fathers to find it decorated with streamers and helium-filled balloons and with a long table with much food.

Hattie was sitting in a big armchair beaming. Her friends, family, and co-workers were there to celebrate with her. But nothing she ever did was just for herself. On a small table next to her, very visible, was a poster asking for money for her to pay her bill at the Second Harvest Food Bank. Authorized food pantries could get food from Second Harvest for a small price per pound. She owed them $241.63, the exact amount of the check Christ Church had to give her!

Sometime before her final illness, Hattie decided to buy the house next door to hers so she could have more room for people to stay with her Shalom Community and space for all the activities. The house was priced low but no one would give her a loan for it because she was a black woman and because, I am sure, they knew the neighborhood might be razed and gentrified before she could get it paid for. Our son, Jim, who loved Hattie and trusted her completely, drove into the city to get Hattie and a couple of her friends to take them to his bank in Hanover Park. His bank agreed to loan her the $20,000 she needed. As it turned out, someone else from another church stepped up and helped her get the money, but she said it was because Jim took that first step in helping God answer her prayer.

Many people who lived in private houses or apartments made regular trips to the laundromat. It was not always a safe place to get to or to be in.

Hattie prayed for a solution to that dangerous situation. A friend of our son Jim was an appliance dealer who had a surplus of outdated but still operational washers and dryers that were taking up room in his storage area. Jim called Hattie and asked her what she was praying for. She said she was praying for washers and dryers. The dealer delivered several to homes where they could be used.

On one occasion Hattie prayed for band uniforms and got not only uniforms but instruments as well. She was chairman of the board of the Paul J. Hall Boys Club and Drum and Bugle Corps. The boys wanted to march in the Bud Billiken parade, the oldest and largest African American parade in the United States. It is the highlight of the year in Bronzeville. The parade, which was started on August 11, 1929, now includes politicians, beauty queens, celebrities, musical performers, and dozens of marching, tumbling, and dancing groups. It has grown from a locally sponsored event to one with major corporate presence. The parade sponsors raise money for college scholarships for local youth.

The problem with getting the drum and bugle corps into the parade was that they couldn't afford suitable uniforms, which in the Bud Billiken Parade were elaborate and colorful. Neither the boys' families or the boys' club sponsors could afford anything that would be appropriate. Hattie prayed for uniforms for them. As happened so often when she prayed, God answered more abundantly than she even asked. A band in a high school in a wealthy white suburb had some old uniforms that they no longer needed. In addition, they had just purchased some new instruments. So along with the uniforms, they also gave their old instruments to the boys. These old ones were better than what the corps already had.

One day we were taking a load of food and clothes to Hattie in Jim's station wagon. On the way, the radiator sprang a leak. We parked in front of Hattie's house with steam and heat pouring out of the engine. After we unloaded the supplies, we visited with Hattie awhile and prayed together, Jim asked Hattie if she had any empty milk jugs that we could fill with water for the trip home. As she filled the jugs she prayed over them. She helped us carry them to the car and prayed over the radiator. We drove the thirty miles home without adding a drop of water and without the steam and heat.

Hattie describes one case of prayers being answered.

Like I said before, I was always the goody two shoes type of lady, always wanting to do something for somebody, and with 5 miles of public housing like Robert Taylor all the way over to the scattered sites of Washington Park homes on Lake front, at Christmas time a lot of children are without toys and whatnot. I had a little office where I was working for the Council for Community Services. I had a little office on 47th St. and one of the things I would do there is let that be a place where people could come and get toys, Christmas baskets, and things like that. I had serviced all the families that I could, and it was Christmas Eve and I sent my secretary home. I was ready to close the door and go home, but there was a big legal pad that I had with two of the largest families listed on there that had nothing. They lived in Robert Taylor.

I said to myself, "Lord." I was talking out loud. I've always had a way of praying without getting on my knees. I just talked to the Lord. I said, "Lord, there's nothing that I can do for them." I was getting ready to go home and fix Christmas dinner, when the phone rang, and there was one of the sisters who worked with me in the past I hadn't heard from her in six months. She said, "Hattie there's a woman who has closed her dry goods store in Bridgeport (a very hostile territory)." She went back to her store and opened her little shop, and said, somebody needs these things, and packed up two great big long cardboard boxes, about four feet square and brought them to the convent at Nativity School and gave them to the sister who had greeted her at the door, and she said, "Sister, I don't know why I did this, but somebody needs these things." Well, it was so late on Christmas Eve that Sister Carol said, I don't know anybody who needs them, but give them to Sister Hattie, and she'll do something with them." Then she asked me if she could bring boxes over. They were filled with everything I had listed on the tablet of paper, and she was in awe, and I was in awe. Here were three women who knew nothing at all about each other. This woman didn't know me, what I had on the list, God used her to fill the list. As I went down the list, everything she had that came out of those two boxes, brand new merchandise, was exactly what was needed. I said, "Sister, look at God." And I was speechless and she was speechless. We just looked at one another. That is walking in faith.[111]

There must have been countless other times just like this when Hattie's prayers were answered with specificity that I don't know about. By the same token, she must have uttered countless prayers that went unanswered. She prayed fervently for the well-being of her children, especially for her drug-addicted son, Bruce, who was homeless and came home only when he was sick. Most certainly she prayed for her neighbors and for her neighborhood as a whole. If these prayers had been answered, Bronzeville would have been a paradise on earth.[112]

Hattie in 1988. Used by permission: Williams Family.

During her final illness, Hattie was in a hospital that was on my way home from my "Bread for the World" office, which was at the Catholic Theological Union in Hyde Park. As I was leaving my office one afternoon, I wanted to stop at the hospital to see her. I counted my money and realized that I didn't have enough to pay for parking at the hospital. I decided I just couldn't go to see her. Despite this, I took the exit from the freeway to the hospital, and right by the front entrance of the hospital was a non-metered, on-street parking place. Such parking is a rarity most any place in Chicago. It was even closer to the main entrance than the expensive parking garage would have been.

I parked and made my way to Hattie's room. When I entered the room, she was sitting in a chair and covered with a colorful afghan. When she saw me she said, "I knew you would come." She had been praying that I would come to visit her that day.

---

111 Edwards, interview, 8.
112 On one of my last visits with her in the hospital, she asked for my prayers that God would protect her from the Devil. Doubting the existence of the devil, I didn't understand how such a faithful servant of God could be worried about assaults from such a being. As I have read the history of the Black Belt in preparation for keeping my promise to Hattie to write this book about her, I am painfully aware that she met the devil head on in many instances in her life. The devil was not in the form of a Lucifer or a demon in a red suit but in the form of the evil of the powers and principalities that were at work in her beloved neighborhood.

In 1968 Hattie had to have another surgery to remove a brain tumor. In 1987 another tumor appeared, but she refused to have another surgery. She had been given a trip to the Holy Land, got as far as New York City, but then had to return home.

After Hattie died in a retirement home in the presence of her family on August 30, 1990, her family wanted to see that a Chicago park near Hattie's house was named for her.

As a final accolade, Bernard Williams Jr., Hattie's eldest son and Hattie's sister, Julia Liddell, were leaders in the effort to get city park #532 named after Hattie. Bernard wrote a biography of her in 2011 to submit to the Board of the Chicago Park District Board of Directors describing the things she had done that would qualify her for such an honor. The family and friends of another community activist, Izora Davis, were lobbying to have the park named after Davis. The park district compromised and named the park The Williams-Davis Park. Dr. Timuel Black presided at the naming ceremony which was held in June 2012. The park is at 4104 South Lake Park, not far from the house where Hattie lived.[113]

Hattie's Park, Naming Ceremony, June 2012. Used by permission: Williams Family.

---

113 See *Chicago Women's Parks and Gardens: Celebrating Significant Chicago Women* (Chicago: Chicago Park District, undated), http://www.chicagowomenspark.com/SIGNIFICANTCHICA-GOWOMEN.php.

Appendix A
MORE WORDS FROM HATTIE

Over the years during which I have been writing this book, I have accumulated so many quotes from Hattie. Some of them I have included in the chapters, but there are stories and ideas that, it seems to me, she would not want left out. I have gathered some of them in this final chapter and arranged them in common themes. They are taken from unpublished interviews by three friends of Hattie's: Father Giani in 1979, Olin Eugene Myers in 1986, and Betsy Edwards in 1988.

SCHOOL DAYS

But living in that particular geographical area [Hyde Park], we were exposed to a better quality of education than we might have got in other areas. I guess I was the only black in my class, during elementary school and high school. Jewish kids were there and if you know about Jewish people, upper income or, the Jewish people they really are the doctors, and the dentists and the business people. So if you're in a classroom setting like that, you'll be motivated and you'll be in competition. I do not find that to be true in the black school system—public school system. There is no competition, and I think that accounts for the low achievement levels of the children in this day and age. I compare what I learned in elementary school and in Hyde Park high school with what my kids—and I'm the mother of six children, now—but I compare what I had as a seventh grade junior high school student with what they learned in their senior year, just such things as the English literature. I got more than they! (Myers)

RACISM

We were very well accepted in the schools here. Although there were twelve of us children, we were very well accepted in the schools here. Along comes the baby girl who was kind of spoiled, you might say, and she wouldn't take some of the insults that we had been conditioned to take even in these schools in an all-white setting.

The books in first grade would read like this: "Spot, I am little, I am black. What am I?" Well, this was Spot, a little dog, but you would have a black kid get up and read this. My sister, Azella, got off on the wrong foot in the same school that we all graduated from. When she hit first grade, she would not read, "I am little. I am black. What am I? I am Spot." You will see that it is a little black dog in the Dick and Jane textbook. But she threw her book down on the floor at six years old and walked out. She was a precocious little brat as far as they were concerned. They kept her at Kenwood until she was ten, and then they told my mother and father that she was incorrigible, and where did you get her from? My mother said, "I got her the same place I got the rest of them." (Edwards)

HER FAITH

My father was an officer in his church, but he was not a minister. In fact, at Olivet Baptist Church they have named a new wing after my father. He was an outstanding concert artist in spite of the fact that he was the father of twelve children and a common laborer at the steel mills and the stockyards. We used to be the largest meatpacking processors in the Midwest. My father was always a man to work, but he had a beautiful, dramatic tenor voice, so he did a lot of fundraising for his church. So I did come up in a Baptist background, but my mother left the Baptist and went Pentecostal, which is still the Protestant background. So with these two constantly warring as to Mom saying that everyone that isn't new Pentecostal faith that she went into, they were going to bust hell wide open, and my dad was saying that heaven was going to be a very small place!

…The reason that I made the decision [to become Catholic] is that I have always been associated with nuns, especially the school sisters at Notre Dame. I have always been interested in children learning to read better, and I remember my days in the PTA when I found that the kids did not have quality of education that I had even in elementary and high school, that we did not have that same motivation in the classrooms, that there was no competition, and I could see the difference in the quality of education.

…And when I was in surgery and was in my recovery period, when I could regain my sight, I remember in 1966 the sisters coming in around my bed with those long black habits and the cross would be hanging from the side and I would say, "They are the ones who prayed me through and surrounded my bed. When I get up from here, Lord, I'm going to take instructions and going to be baptized and confirmed, and by my own choice I am going into the Catholic Church. (Edwards, 1988)

When I was recovering at Michael Reese Hospital, the sisters of Notre Dame, Catholic order, who'd been working with me in the tutoring program that was burned up —the Eleanor Roosevelt study center. It was named that because I had received an award from the Eleanor Roosevelt Memorial Foundation. Well, these nuns were with me. Even at the hospital. They were praying for my recovery. And I felt that that was the place I belong. I felt that I wanted a quieter way of serving God. I never liked the hooping [sic] and hollering and shouting that had gone on in my childhood. I've always liked the quieter way I used to say when I was a kid, "surely there's a quieter way of worshiping God, than beating a tambourine, and somebody yelling, and shouting and falling out, you know. I just didn't see where that was necessary. And I felt that coming into the Catholic Church, I was coming to people—the nuns who had befriended me. I feel that they've been in my life for a purpose, before I was ever Catholic. They never preach to me, they never said nothing to me about the church or anything else. That was my decision, on a bed of affliction, I cast my lot there.

…At that time I knew nothing about the Catholic traditions such as the feast days of different saints. But I had asked the Lord to give me a sign, if I'm doing the right thing. And I later found in studying the life of St. Ambrose, that the feast day of Saint Ambrose fell on December 7, which is my birthday, so that was my sign that I felt that I had joined the right church.

PERSECUTION

Many times my life has been threatened. A tutorial project storefront was burned to the ground by a politician. People felt it a threat for us to get together. I also became aware that it was not a Christ center. That even though it was a good project, I would have to stay on my knees and pray about it. To do God's will instead of mine. (Father Giani)

I suffered persecution when I ran for the office of alderman. So I learned a lot from it and I don't regret it, and I gave the alderman—the regular machine candidate— really hard time. But I learned from it that I would never be active politically again. I thought I was doing a good thing because I was asked, I had sons—and you see, politics is a dirty business. My husband had never been in jail. He was a man, I tell you, in civil service. He worked for the government. But if he would walk the dog—we had a German Shepherd—if he would walk that dog, he would be stopped and searched by the police.

I have a son who's never been in jail. Bernard, Junior. And he was arrested the night before the election. It came out in the *Sun-Times* paper: 'Fourth Ward candidate's son arrested with live ammunition.' He was a soldier returning from, he was in the Army for three years. And he had on this belt and it had bullets around it. And so that's why he was arrested. He didn't have a gun. But live ammunition. See? So thought came to me, I'm getting a double message. You don't deal in politics if you're not ready to stand the heat. I felt that while I couldn't be touched, my men folks would bear the repercussions of anything political that I was in, so I would never get in it again just because I had too many others to pay for what I could do. I had too many men folks to pay the price. They would be the ones that pay. So I left it alone. I just mentioned that to say that sometimes in your efforts to do good, you might make some mistakes. (Myers)

INFLUENCE OF CHURCHES IN THE NEIGHBORHOOD

People don't see the Catholic Church in a positive way. I mean the masses of people. There are individuals that do see it as positive. People think the Catholic Church may give them a handout. They have an attitude that the Catholic Church has a better education system for their children, but they can't afford it. These are the two outstanding things. They also feel that we worship statues. This is due to their lack of understanding.

The Protestant churches in the area are close to the community. They relate to their own members but not to the outside community and their social problems. Many churches in the area have parishioners that do not live in the area. It is part of the black culture to continue attending your original church even if you move. This of course doesn't mean that they owe anything to their particular geographical boundary.

The ministers are selfish and only think in terms of their Sunday offerings. In many ways they conduct their church like a cult. They have a lot of women that have no male or husband in their homes and they like a dictatorship kind of rule that kind of psychological thing that they require a strong male dominance, in the church if nowhere else. So therefore, we do not have any recreational programs, social service organization[s] that will really help in the condition that are speaking about in the black Protestant church. (Father Giani)

ECUMENICAL ACTIVITY

There is some ecumenical activity. I see a small gain initially. Already the presence of Shalom Community is being felt in the area. Some time out of curiosity people who belong to the various churches will say, could you come to explain to us about Shalom Ministry? What is it? People are getting clothes and shoes and they say there is much prayer or they say come and share their sorrows or troubles. In some way they feel that it is a sincere effort and the community is looking for sincerity. They have been used in so many ways by the politicians or in many ways they feel short-changed throughout the education system. The welfare department is an example: they give cost of living raises their employees or government people. Our welfare system hasn't been given a cost of living raise to recipients in seven years. There was a push by people in Shalom and outside of Shalom. We did get a 5% increase [illegible] added income through the Chicago Housing Authority and the high-rise project either your rent goes up, or your taxes and what have you. We pay 6% sales tax on a dollar value. So where is your fight? The thing is that the people have been used and exploited that they look upon the Shalom Community as offering a ray of hope that the people are for real. There is very little that is for real so in our approach to begin to initiate what we call an umbrella we want to service that umbrella for social services. Maybe one church focus is to work with Father Clement at Holy Angels for the employment efforts to enhance what he has already begun there. If the church that has a social service such as Grant Memorial at 4017 Drexel. If we could in some way find a way to implement and work with that Methodist Church regarding the opening of that community center regarding the coming together of the people getting their missionary groups involved in the community working with the senior citizens or the elderly if it's not more than doing something with that person if it once a week or month and giving them a specific point. That is one component one be responsible for. Many of the Protestants have large missionary groups and their idea of missionary work may be to take magazines to a prison or something of that nature and they are beautiful in their white uniforms. They have not gotten them dirty. They have not thought about some elderly person that may need their hair combed or some finger nails cut or just coming in once a week and writing that letter or to pray or read something for them. Getting into the community is one way we want to give something to specific task and not spell it out but ask them what they feel comfortable with this or that or the other, give them options give them choices but this is what we want to do to service the community. (Father Giani)

HIGH-RISE PUBLIC HOUSING BUILDINGS

Another problem we face is the high-rise buildings. Ten families on each floor. Seventeen story buildings [illegible]. Not unusual to have seventy to one hundred children on one floor. Then mothers with teenage children are active sexually so there are more babies in the house. Then if drugs like valium are given you have a problem with black on black crime. When a girl or a woman is raped she just takes a bath and shuts up because if she goes to the hospital she is questioned to see if you were seriously raped. It is dehumanizing.

These are some problems as I see it. No incentive for our young who already have low esteem due to lack of reading ability. Have had no exposure outside the community. No base of comparison.

People are afraid to leave the area. Their fear of the unknown, no way, no offer nor opportunity to leave the area. Some try to do this but even fail due to education and health. (Father Giani)

This is the mechanism of the city, the government. The next step would be, it would not be hard to come into houses such as this and condemn it. Just condemn the house. Find something wrong with it, even if it's a nonexistent wrong. They would find some way to say, "Oh, this is unfit for human habitation, we condemn it. Now, we've assessed your property, and it ain't worth nothing. Here, just $5000 for nuisance value. Now get out of here." And then they redevelop this whole area.

About the high-rise public housing: Well, they claim that they're going to be rehabbed, and those who qualify will be allowed to return to the lakefront. "Those who qualify." When I hear that kind of rhetoric, then I want to know what's the criteria for returning. So it's a big question there—and I could be wrong. But I do not see this, as it is, the only lake front in a slum area, where you're right on Lake Michigan. This is choice land, and I just don't think we're long for this neighborhood. I think we got in here after World War II. During World War II this was a concentration camp for Japanese.

I'm using strong language—it wasn't like a concentration camp but it was. They were not allowed to leave here for the duration of World War II.

See before that time it was whites. But then you see, for some reason during World War II this became highly populated with Japanese. After World War II, well, then blacks were allowed to take over. Well, the houses are very old here, built in 1897. So you see, they were done for then. Then if we buy them and then can't get any loans or anything to rehab, well, then that means that we deteriorate and that's why many times people look at what blacks buy and say, "Now they don't even keep up their property, you know, they just let it go." But it really is by design. The suppression is there—this institutionalized racism that really exists. It just suppresses the people. And so some of the blacks claimed that this is racism to remove them from the Lakefront. So they had a pretty good coverage on television. (Myers)

PUBLIC EDUCATION

The unified effort was something that would be lacking now, but in those days of the 60s, during the civil rights movement, during the lifetime of Dr. King. Even the ministers, the churches, which now have regressed in this particular geographical area, that they don't feel that they owe anything to the remnant of the people in the community unless they're members of their church. We've come full swing to that kind of thinking now, as far as these churches around the neighborhood. They will not feel any responsibility for the community as whole. It's their parishioners. But not in those days. There was a sense of unity among blacks, that was inspiring, exciting, and we found that we could use Ebenezer Baptist Church for the Freedom Schools. But we could use other churches for an afterschool tutorial program. So we boycotted the Board of Education and I coordinated that boycott in this geographical area—clear every school. There was no school.

We established what we called "Freedom Schools." We had Freedom Schools where we even had just volunteers just working with the kids.

See, and we said, "Down with Willis!" And so we got rid of Willis, but we have a lot to learn. But just imagine how I've learned that you cannot remove the general superintendent of schools and expect to bring about a change. But I had a lot to learn—I was enthused, I was honest and I was sincere. But in ridding the schools of a superintendent, I see, I must confess, things are in a sorrier state today than they were in the 1960s.

You know it's just little concessions here and there, but I'm saying, superficial but I could tell you why I say that there is a regression. I do not see where integration of the school system will ever take place, but I see where our better teachers in the low-income black communities are sort of siphoned off and put in to integrate white schools. So the cream is siphoned off, so they were left with full-time-basis substitute teachers and people who have been completely demoralized by the system. You gotta believe in what you're doing—got to have something there. And that spark is missing in many cases. (Myers)

MARTIN LUTHER KING JR.

So what I'm saying is, Daley didn't want Martin Luther King Jr. in Chicago, and many of the black ministers who were straight Democrat people—they were part of the Democrat machine—for the rewards, for the concessions, for the patronage jobs, they would go to their parishioners in the church. They all rejected Dr. King.

[She gives as an example the pastor of her father's church.] I didn't know how vehement he was until. During those days, and my father was a member of that church for 45 years—in fact they built a new wing down there and it's named after my father. So I remember a recital, and he was alive, my father was alive during the Civil Rights Movement and I was passing a flyer that Dr. Martin Luther King Jr. would be at Soldier Field. We were going to have a rally. And so during intermission I just happened to be giving people these flyers and then the minister's wife said, "I am going to tell your father what you are doing down here, and we don't allow this mess at Olivet," and so she pulled all the flyers right out of people's hands and people were just standing aghast, and she's taking back these little half page flyers about Dr. King. So these are the kinds of situations that--I'm talking about grassroots level--that went on during that time. But many people really rallied behind Dr. King in prayer. They didn't know anything else to do. Many of us who could do a little more, we did. I think that it still stands to this day that many of us realize what the coming of Dr. Martin Luther King Jr. meant to the human race. There are other people who are benefiting from everything he stood for.

Now maybe I'm wrong. I'm not an authority. This I could see it from grass root level the city, and I could name the most prominent churches, where ministers would get up and say, "Well, you know, Dr. King did well in the South, but he does not know the North and when you hear a prominent leadership go through this, well, I mean all of these people are sitting there and some of them will say, "Amen, yeah, he's a wonderful man, but he should've stayed in the South—he ain't got no business coming up here North." That's following the leader. That's what I saw many black leaders. But I would say that they were in a minority. I'm not going to throw that at all black leadership I could be totally wrong.

I took part in the rally at Soldier Field. My participation was to be there, to bring people there and also to distribute the flyers, throughout this neighborhood and anywhere else that I could. So that was the extent of my participation. I did not march in Cicero, against the housing. I remember Dr. King at the rally, as usual, he has that charisma, and he gave a speech. He explained his presence in Chicago, why he was here. And I noticed —the reason I guess that I participated, even at that small level—is I noticed there was such hostility coming from unlikely places, such as outstanding civic leaders, politicians, in fact they were in opposition to Dr. King's even coming to Chicago. They made the statements that he was okay in the South but he had no business coming up here North. And so I felt I had to defend that position, because I felt that he had every right to be here.

I listened to everything Dr. King had said—I listened to speeches, I watched how he was criticized, and I always just felt that that was the truth, and his whole philosophy and that's what it stood for. And I still feel that. But the persistence that he had—I wanted some of it. And I do believe I have some of it. (Myers)

BLACK HISTORY MONTH

The one thing that I would like to see happen out of this is for Black History to become part of American History. I don't like it when there is Black History Month in February. "Okay, let's talk about the niggers this month." Now the rest of the time, say nothing. And this is the attitude, in many of our situations Work it into regular history, you know, all of a sudden during the civil rights movement we were told, oh we were going to have black history, so then they would give a quickie course to a white teacher, you know, and then this white teacher's supposed to go back and teach black history. A quickie course, you know? You can't do it that way.

SURGERIES

My first brain surgery was on March 15, 1966. And the second one was five years ago, that would've been in March, 1981…At that time I was struggling to live, and I was in a very bad situation. I started losing my lateral vision and didn't know what was happening. It was pressure on the optic nerve. I lost the lateral vision, then I just lost my sight. I was very sick and I had this operation. I just prayed to the Lord at that time to let me live, because this area was the center of gang activity, like the Blackstone Rangers, the Devil's Disciples, and it was a bloodbath among blacks at that time, very similar to what is happening to Hispanics in Humboldt Park. This was Stone territory, Blackstone territory, and I had five boys, little fellows, and I wanted to live to see them grow up. So I prayed and made vows to the Lord to serve him and serve my fellow man if he would let me live to raise the children. I had faith to believe so as I went into surgery at Michael Reese I remember taking with me the 23rd Psalm. The part, "Yea, though I walk through the valley of the shadow of death, I will fear no evil." That was in my mind. I don't remember anything until I came to in the recovery room, and intensive care, I could finish that Psalm. I remember thanking the Lord. I had to have radiation for 30 days following the surgery because of the removal of tumors. This was prescribed and I remember that it would almost take my consciousness. It kind of makes you ill when you have a lot of x-ray being beamed right on the brain. They cut off the legs of this chair in the therapy unit so that I was seated almost on the floor while they beamed this x-ray into my head and I remember thinking, Lord, I will serve you. I will go and serve you. Please, Lord, let me keep my right mind. Give me the activity of my limbs, let my tongue praise you. And when I got up from there, I had this purpose in my mind, who is my fellow man?

Appendix B
NEPHEW'S MEMORIES

My Aunt Hattie Williams

By

Dr. Clifton Hunt

June, 29, 2017

As a child my aunt Hattie Williams was very influential in my life. At the age of 6 years olds she would tell me stories of how I prayed for her when she had a brain tumor and the Lord healed her from the tumor. When I was eight years old, my aunt Hattie saw the God given ability that was nurtured by my mother to play the piano by ear. My aunt Hattie fold me a sponsor who paid for me to take music lessons at the American Conservatory of Music in Chicago Illinois. At the American Conservatory of Music I learned to read music and play classical music starting at the ages of 8 years old until I was 13 years old.

When I was having problems in elementary school and failed the second grade, my Aunt Hattie found me a Catholic Priest who tutored me. I was able to make a double in seventh grade and graduated from eighth grade in summer school. Because of my Aunt Hattie's intervention, I was able to start my freshmen year of high school on time. However, I messed-up in high school and dropped out. Once again my aunt Hattie found me a tutor, the materials I needed, and the site where I could go and take the GED test. Because of my aunt Hattie's' help I was able to pass the GED test the first time.

After graduating from high school, Aunt Hattie found me another sponsor and I returned to the American Conservatory of Music. I competed in competitions and received several awards for my God given musical gift of playing the piano. While I was majoring at the American Conservatory of Music as a classical pianist, after two years my sponsorship ended. Aunt Hattie helped me fill out the paper work to receive a scholarship to attend Kennedy King College where I received my Associate of Art Degree. After graduating from Kennedy King College, I continued my studies and attended Chicago State University where I received a scholarship and graduated with a Bachler of Art Degree in education with a focus in music.

Because of the foundation that was set by my aunt Hattie and my hunger for knowledge, I continued my education and enrolled in Roosevelt University where I received my Master of Art Degree with a focus on curriculum and instruction as well as received my educational leadership/administration certification. I continued my studies at Roosevelt University and completed all my classwork for my Doctor of Education Degree. However, because I was so overwhelmed by my new positions as a Curriculum Coordinator and Principalship at Chicago Public Schools, I did not write my dissertation. Once again because of the foundation started by my aunt Hattie I enrolled in Olivet University where I graduated with my Doctor of Education Degree on May 6, 2017. Because of the love and support I received from my aunt Hattie, I am now Dr. Clifton Hunt.

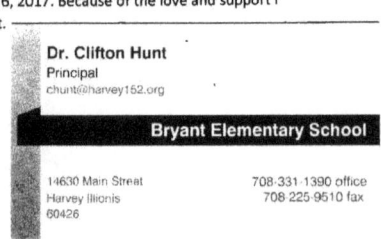

My name is David C. Kay and I am the nephew of Hattie Williams. As a child, I did not realize the powerful influence and care that my aunt Hattie had for humanity; however, when I graduated from high school and joined the armed forces, I saw the love and concern for justice that was in her heart.

Although I was employed through the family business, I decided to join the armed forces [U.S. Army] and learn a trade listed as "71 Lima" [Administrative Specialist]. I went through my basic training with flying colors, and then went to advanced training where the army was to prepare me for the job I signed up for. During advanced training, I went to take the typing test however because of poor training I failed the minimum of 45 words per minute, I was given two weeks to pass a makeup test, but I was not trained by a teacher, I had to go for myself in a class room with all the rest, consequently I failed and the armed forces determined I was only good for the job title of "11 Bravo" [Infantry soldier]. I was shipped off the Fort Benning Ga to be trained for battle; however, with my religious background I entered the army as a conscientious objector to war, I just wanted to be trained as promised for 71 Lima.

Some way somehow, my Aunt Hattie heard of my situation and she got in touch with me to get the particulars, she then explained to me my rights as a U.S. citizen. I can remember her saying on the phone "son you don't have to stand for this you have rights and the Government has violated your rights".

Before I knew it, there was a letter from them Senator Paul Simon, Senator Stevens, and others that wrote in my defense as a conscientious objector and I was honorably discharged from the Armed forces. Who knows what would have happened if my aunt Hattie Williams was not there for me with her loving concerned heart for humanity.

I will always be grateful for God's gift to me of Hattie Kay Williams.

Respectfully Submitted

David C. Kay

Richard

ACKNOWLEDGEMENTS

I say that we are threads in God's tapestry, and if we can be bent and interwoven, the finished product will be to his glory.

Betsy Edwards

These words, spoken by Hattie, are a perfect expression of my experience writing this book and as an acknowledgment and thanks to all the people who have been involved in its production.

My thanks go to Keaka Stokes, Hattie's great-niece, for finding me online and thereby connecting me to Hattie's sister, Julia Kay Liddell. The personal information about Hattie's life and the photographs of her and her family came from Julia, who worked with great love and diligence to find them for me. During these years, Julia has become a dear and revered friend.

Thanks also to the dedicated genealogists who knew how and where to search for family history that I would never have found: Don Kay, Chris Forrest, and Chet Henry. Being able to trace Hattie's ancestry from 1831 onward was a great help in understanding her in ways that otherwise would have been impossible.

A special thanks goes to Michael Harris, who found sources and people online that I had not found. Because of his research, I was able to obtain the interviews of Hattie from Olin Eugene Myers and Roger Schroeder, which helped Hattie to come alive in the book.

Mrs. Beverly Cook, Assistant Curator of the Vivian G. Harsh Research Collection of Afro-American History and Literature at the Woodson Branch of the Chicago Public Library, carried boxes and boxes of documents to Julia Liddell and me when I was in Chicago to do research.

It may be that the most painful thing a writer must do is have other people read the manuscript in its earliest forms. So, for their patience and enthusiasm and criticism, I thank Jim Phillips, Bonny Henry, Chris Forest, Linda Risseeuw, Deborah Hall, and Lawn Griffiths. And a special thanks to my copy editor Karen Ketchaver, cover designer Holly Silcox, layout editor Jaime Briceno, and editor Melody Layton McMahon.

All along the way, there have been countless people who have heard me tell "Hattie stories" and have been inspired by them. I thank them for listening and for being inspired by her.

My husband, Norm, my son, Jim, and my daughter, Nancy, were part of Hattie's story as it unfolded in our lives. Through all these years of the writing of the book, they have added stories and been helpfully critical and amazingly patient, filling a special role in the whole project.

BIBLIOGRAPHY

Alexander, Michelle. *The New Jim Crow: Mass Incarceration in the Age of Colorblindness*. New York: New Press, 2012.

Anderson, Alan B. and George W. Pickering. *Confronting the Color Line: The Broken Promise of the Civil Rights Movement in Chicago*. Athens: University of Georgia Press, 2007.

Baker, Ray Stannard. *Following the Color Line: An Account of Negro Citizenship in the American Democracy*. New York: Doubleday Page, 1908.

Baldwin, Davarian L. *Chicago's New Negroes: Modernity, the Great Migration and Black Urban Life*. University of North Carolina Press Chapel Hill, 2007.

Bevans, Stephen, Eleanor Doidge, and Robert Schreiter, eds. *The Healing Circle, Essays in Cross-Cultural Mission, Presented to the Rev. Dr. Claude Marie Barbour*. Chicago: CCGM Publications, 2000.

Biles, Roger. *Richard J. Daley: Politics, Race, and the Governing of Chicago*. Dekalb, IA: Northern Illinois University Press, 1995.

Black, Timuel D. Jr. *Bridges of Memory: Chicago's First Generation of Black Migration*. Chicago: Northwestern University Press, 2008.

———. *Bridges of Memory: Chicago's Second Generation of Black Migrants*. Chicago: Northwestern University Press, 2007.

Christie, Ron. *Acting White: The Curious History of a Racial Slur*. New York: St. Martin's, 2010.

Cooley, Will. "Moving Up, Moving Out: Racial Mobility in Chicago 1914-1972." PhD diss., University of Illinois, 2008.

Danns, Dionne. *Something Better for Our Children: Black Organization in the Chicago Public Schools, 1963-1971*. Studies in African American History and Culture. New York: Routledge, 2001.

Drake, St. Clair and Horace R. Cayton. *Black Metropolis: A Study of Life in a Northern City.* Chicago: University of Chicago Press, 1970.

Dubois, W. E. B. *The Souls of Black Folk.* New York: Barnes and Noble, 2003. Originally published in 1903.

Frick, Lisa, ed. *Teen Pregnancy and Parenting.* Current Controversies Series. Detroit: Greenhaven, 2006.

Grossman, James R. *Land of Hope: Chicago, Black Southerners and the Great Migration.* Chicago: University of Chicago Press, 1989.

Harris-Perry, Melissa V. *Sister Citizen: Shame, Stereotypes, and Black Women in America.* New Haven: Yale University Press, 2011.

Hays, Sharon. *Flat Broke with Children: Women in the Era of Welfare Reform.* New York: Oxford University Press, 2003.

Hirsch, Arnold Richard. *Making the Second Ghetto: Race and Housing in Chicago, 1940-1960.* Chicago: University of Chicago Press, 1983.

Homel, Michael W. *Down from Equality: Black Chicagoans and the Public Schools, 1920-1941.* Urbana: University of Illinois Press, 1984.

Hunt, D. Bradford. *Blueprint for Disaster: The Unraveling of Chicago Public Housing.* Chicago: University of Chicago Press, 2005.

Hurston, Zora Neale. *Their Eyes Were Watching God.* New York: Harper Collins, 2000. Original copyright, 1937.

Kennedy, Randall. *The Persistence of the Color Line: Racial Politics and the Obama Presidency.* New York: Vintage, 2011.

Materson, Lisa G. *For the Freedom of Her Race: Black Women and Electoral Politics in Illinois 1877-1932. Chapel Hill: University of North Carolina Press, 2009.

Satter, Beryl. *Family Properties: Race, Real Estate and the Exploitation of Black Urban America*. New York: Henry Holt, 2009.

Seligman, Amanda I. *Block by Block: Neighborhoods and Public Policy on Chicago's West Side*. Chicago: University of Chicago Press, 2005.

Sitkoff, Harvard. *The Struggle for Black Equality, 1954-1992*. New York: Hill and Wang, 1993.

———. *Toward Freedom Land, The Long Struggle for Racial Equality*. Lexington: University of Kentucky Press, 2010.

Spear, Allan H. *Black Chicago: The Making of a Negro Ghetto, 1890-1920*. Chicago: University of Chicago Press, 1968.

Stead, William T. *If Christ Came to Chicago: A Plea for the Union of All Who Love in the Service of All Who Suffer*. Bibliolife: Historical Reproduction of the book first published in 1894.

Tuttle, William M. Jr. *Race Riot: Chicago In the Red Summer of 1919*. New York: Atheneum, 1982.

Vankatesh, Sudhir Alladi. *Gang Leader for a Day: A Rogue Sociologist Takes to the Streets*. New York: Penguin Press, 2008.

———. *Off the Books: The Underground Economy of the Urban Poor*. Cambridge, MA: Harvard University Press, 2006.

Waskow, Arthur. *From Race Riot to Sit-In, 1919 and the 1960s*. New York: Doubleday, 1966.

White, Deborah Gray. *Too Heavy a Load: Black Women in Defense of Themselves, 1894-1994*. New York: W.W. Norton, 1999.

Woodward, C. Vann. *The Strange Career of Jim Crow: A Commemorative Edition with a New Afterward by William S. McFeely*. New York: Oxford, 2002.

www.ingramcontent.com/pod-product-compliance
Lightning Source LLC
LaVergne TN
LVHW090116080426
835507LV00040B/901